THE SONG OF SONGS

THE SONG
OF SONGS

TRANSLATED AND
INTERPRETED AS A
DRAMATIC POEM BY
LEROY WATERMAN

ANN ARBOR
UNIVERSITY OF MICHIGAN PRESS
1948

WITHDRAWN

TO

those students of the Department of Oriental Languages
and Literatures and of other departments of the University of Michigan and its Extension Service
with whom, during the past thirty years,
I have had the privilege and pleas-
ure of reading and discussing
the Song of Songs, this
little volume is af-
fectionately

DEDICATED

PREFACE

THE haunting beauty and the irrepressible charm of the poetry of the Song of Songs persist undimmed, regardless of all theories as to the basic meaning of the entire poem. That very fact will probably never permit interpretation of the Song to rest until a rendition has been achieved that accounts adequately for all its features, and the lure of the quest for such a rendition must be the justification for the present work. It is an added incentive that the charm and beauty of the poem may well prove more and more compelling as that aim is more nearly approximated.

The challenging criticisms and the kindly encouragement of colleagues in the field of Old Testament study and in other fields have both urged me on in this endeavor and greatly aided me. I wish to mention particularly Professor Charles C. Torrey, of Yale University, Principal W. R. Taylor, of University College, University of Toronto, and Dean Luther A. Weigle, of Yale Divinity School.

I am much indebted to Professor Herbert C. Youtie and Professor DeWitt H. Parker, of the University of Michigan, who read the manuscript and made many valuable comments.

Grateful acknowledgment is due the Horace H. Rackham School of Graduate Studies of the University of Michigan for undertaking publication of this work. I desire also to express my appreciation to Dr. Eugene S. McCartney, Editor of Scholarly Publications of the University of Michigan, for reading the manuscript and making helpful suggestions, and, more especially, to Miss Grace E. Potter, Associate Editor in the same office, for furnishing invaluable aid in the detailed editing and clarification of the manuscript and for seeing it through the press.

L. WATERMAN

vii

CONTENTS

Cover.—The lines of script on the cover are excerpts from the famous "Gezer" calendar, which has been called the oldest extant form of Hebrew writing. The Song of Songs was presumably written for centuries in a similar script. The lines read: "The month of sowing"; "The month of late sowing"; "The month of pruning"; "The month of summer fruits." These are the seasons that figure so largely in the Song.

NOTE

All citations of the Song of Songs refer, unless otherwise
noted, to the rendering in the present volume; other Biblical
references are to the American Revised Version. Letters in
these citations indicate lines.

INTRODUCTION

ALTHOUGH numerous studies have been devoted to the Song of Songs, no single view of it and no one interpretation have received general acceptance.[1] Nor has any interpretation thus far proposed dealt adequately with its entire contents, for virtually all accounts have required either that certain features be left out or that others be assumed. The following statement by H. H. Rowley illustrates the situation: "The view I adopt finds in it nothing but what it appears to be, lovers' songs, expressing their delight in one another and the warm emotion of their hearts."[2] Actually, as will be shown, slightly less than half the Song complies with that description.

The first known classification of this purely secular poem was made about 100 A.D. by Josephus, who placed it among "the hymns to God." That classification immediately indicates a highly figurative, rather than a literal, interpretation of the Song, and it was its allegorical interpretation that indubitably made possible its canonization as a part of Holy Scripture.

The Jews began the transformation by seeing in the maiden a symbol of Israel and by taking Solomon to mean God. The Christians accepted the Song in this sense, along with its inclu-

[1] R. H. Pfeiffer, *Introduction to the Literature of the Old Testament* (New York, 1941), p. 714.

[2] "Interpretation of the Song of Songs," *Journal of Theological Studies,* 38 (1937): 362.

I

sion in the Old Testament. It remained for Origen, in the third century of our era, to provide the classic form of the allegory for Christians by changing God and Israel to Christ and the Church, respectively. This interpretation has continued to find expression to the present day in the running heads of the King James version of the Song. Since, however, there is nothing in the poem to encourage its being construed in this fashion, and since, moreover, no consistent allegory for the entire Song has ever been formulated (for example, if the maiden represents the Church, who are the sixty queens and the eighty concubines of Christ's harem?), it is no wonder that a literal interpretation has finally prevailed.

Explanation of the Song as a survival of an early liturgy of the fertility cult has been advanced in recent times, notably by T. J. Meek and by W. Wittekindt.[3] This interpretation is now expressed in the rendering of the Song in *The Bible, An American Translation* (1927). It is a reversion to the theory that the poem is an allegory, but one whose original significance was unknown to the Hebrews who were responsible for its present form. The objections to the allegorical approach in general are no less applicable here.

But with the development of a literal interpretation, beginning in the fifteenth century and culminating in our time, we reach the present impasse of irreconcilable diversity of opinion as to the nature and the intention of the poem. There are two general points of view: first, that it is in some true sense an entity; and, second, that it has no organic unity, but is merely a collection of short, detached love lyrics.

Among those who hold the first view of the Song its dramatic quality has been stressed. There is a two-character arrangement

---

[3] T. J. Meek, "The Song of Songs and the Fertility Cult" in *The Song of Songs, A Symposium,* edited by W. H. Schoff (Philadelphia, 1924); W. Wittekindt, *Das Hohe Lied und seine Beziehungen zum Istarkult* (Hannover, 1926).

and a three-character arrangement, sometimes with divisions into acts and scenes. The poem is entirely lacking in stage directions, however, as well as in any formal indication of the speakers; moreover, the proposed scenes are too brief and artificial to be convincing, regardless of the fact that drama, as such, is otherwise unknown in Hebrew literature. The attempt in the last century, particularly by Franz Delitzsch[4] in his commentary on the Song, to treat the two-character theory as representing historical events failed because it required the withdrawal of Solomon from his throne to become a rustic shepherd.

Among those who regard the Song as a collection of detached lyrics there are two general attitudes. One of these is exemplified in the so-called "Syrian-wedding" theory formulated by K. Budde[5] and C. Siegfried[6] on the basis of the observations of J. G. Wetzstein[7] on wedding customs in Syria in 1865. But that the work is not just a collection of wedding songs should be clear from the fact that over fifty verses center about a lover who is absent and who cannot be reached.[8] The other view maintains that the poems were gathered together solely because of their common topic—love. Various overlappings and intermixtures of the two views are advocated. None of these explanations, however, are able to account for all the materials of the Song; that it is not just erotic poetry would appear evident in that 85 verses out of 117 represent dialogues between women.

A concise yet comprehensive historical résumé indicating the character and diversity of the interpretations of the Song may be found in the brochure by H. H. Rowley.[9] It may be said that

---

[4] *Commentary on the Song of Songs and Ecclesiastes* (Edinburgh, 1877).
[5] "The Song of Solomon," *New World*, March, 1894, pp. 56–77.
[6] *Prediger und Hoheslied* (Göttingen, 1898).
[7] "Die syrische Dreschtafel," *Bastian's Zeitschrift für Ethnologie*, 5 (1873): 270–302.
[8] Cf. Pfeiffer, *op. cit.*, p. 709.   [9] *Op. cit.*, pp. 337–363.

3

two of the chief factors that have hitherto frustrated all efforts to regard the Song as a single unit have been the apparent uncertainty as to the speakers and the persons addressed and the lack of any clear sequence in time or place such as would be expected from the presence of Solomon. Attempts to treat the work as a conglomerate have failed to furnish a hypothesis that accounts adequately either for the nuclei proposed or for the recurrent indications of a basic material common to the whole poem.

To admit that irreconcilable diversity of interpretation of the Song still prevails is not to deny that some advance has been made. The very fact that earlier as well as more recent theories and proposals have been steadily and decisively challenged has undoubtedly had a salutary clarifying effect.

EVIDENCE OF RECENSIONS

Of positive gains that have been made in interpretation perhaps the most far-reaching is the recognition that the Song has come to us in a "Jerusalem recension of much earlier northern poems."[10] The full import of that insight has, however, not been realized or taken into account.

In view of this possible clue to the original a certain amount of "form" criticism, to use the phrase in a most general sense, is a necessary precaution before a thesis may be ventured in regard to the Song as a whole. As a first consideration we have to note that this so-called "Jerusalem recension" is transmitted in our present Masoretic text, and that that text is, therefore, our only immediately available source for the Song. Nevertheless, we know that behind our text lies the much older consonantal form, and the possibility that it underwent a distinct

[10] See J. A. Bewer, *Introduction to Old Testament Literature* (New York, 1924), p. 393; cf. Otto Eissfeldt, *Einleitung in das Alte Testament* (Tübingen, 1934), p. 535.

recension. A vowelless text, such as that in which the Song was unquestionably transmitted for centuries, lends itself, especially if committed to strangers, to more or less aberration from the original words and meaning, and hence the vowel pointing, as well as the order of the text, calls for more than usually careful scrutiny. Particularly is caution needed in view of the fact that different political and geographic backgrounds may result in widely different estimates of an outstanding national figure such as Solomon.

In North Israel, for example, Solomon was probably the most hated of all rulers and rightly regarded as the prime cause of the breakup of the kingdom; in the literature of the North that dealt with him, therefore, we could hardly look for anything short of dislike and disparagement. In Judah, on the other hand, the presence of Solomon in the Song was from the first regarded as its most significant feature (1: 1), and it would be only natural to expect that a Judean would make every effort to interpret his rôle there in an honorable light, that is, one that accorded with his traditional dignity and glory.

How can the possibility of such regional editing of the text be checked, so that this activity may be correctly appraised?

One suggestion is that a late gloss may sometimes throw light on the original. In 1: 1, for example, the expression "which to Solomon" has for a considerable time been widely accepted as a gloss, first, because of the longer form of the relative particle, a form which never occurs in the poem, and, secondly, because no one has succeeded in maintaining Solomon's authorship.

It may be doubted whether the glossator intended to convey the idea of authorship, since in no other ascription of authorship, either to Solomon or to others, in the Old Testament does this particular phrasing occur. The most that it clearly says is that the work pertains to Solomon, that is, it deals with him. If the poem

dealt in any way with Solomon when it came to the attention of
the Judeans (which may well have been at the time of the
fall of North Israel), they were bound to emphasize that fact
because of the high regard for him in the South; the gloss "which
to Solomon" would therefore indicate that he had occupied a place
in the Song from the beginning. And this conclusion remains
valid regardless of the unity or the heterogeneity of the poem's
content. Moreover, attempts to remove Solomon's name from
the poem on metrical grounds have not been convincing.[11]

Further proof that the depiction of Solomon in the Song was
present from the first and was of Northern origin is to be found
in the fact that he is not its hero.[12] Even when the evidence is
weighted in favor of such a thesis it is apparent that his rôle
is a minor one; he speaks fewer than one fifth of the verses in the
book, and after 7:9 he is lost to view—the work ends, as it begins
in the traditional version, without regard to him.

Had Solomon's presence in the poem been from the start a
Southern element, whether in the original or as a later addition, it
is incredible that he would have been introduced so briefly and
that none of the wisdom, power, and splendor traditionally associated with him would have been recorded. It is no less incredible that his rôle would have been limited to paying compliments to a young woman whose rank is not specified and who is
unidentified by him except in so far as he insists that she was
unusually beautiful. For a man who was reputed to have a
thousand women in his harem (1 Kings 11:3), seven hundred of
them princesses, the episodes in which he figures in the Song are
not of a character to add luster to his name. The apparent in-
definiteness of his relationship to the girl he addresses has, on the
contrary, the effect of presenting Solomon as, at best, a somewhat
jaded (6:8) and repetitious coquet (1:15; 4:1–3; 6:5–7).

[11] Robert Gordis, "A Wedding Song for Solomon," *Journal of Biblical Literature*, 63 (1944):264–266.　　　[12] *Ibid.*, p. 265.

The original attitude of the Song toward Solomon, while it need not be expected to coincide with these indications of character, can be accurately determined only from a study of the unpointed text as a whole. But inasmuch as that attitude now appears to have been Northern, it is bound to have affected decidedly the larger aspects of the original form of the Song.

Time and place settings, as well as glosses, may be important factors in the recovery of an original text, for they are inevitably bound up with literary form. A time setting is at least implied by the introduction of Solomon. A place setting may be deduced from the presence in the Song of a group of characters referred to as the "daughters of Jerusalem." It is of considerable importance to such a deduction that the identity of this group be determined as nearly as possible. The occasion for the appearance of these women and their function in the Song should be noted.

In 3:11 the "daughters of Jerusalem" are summoned to meet King Solomon. Clearly the summons was no general announcement to the populace, since only women were specified. Nor was it addressed to all the women of the city, for that would have required an assemblage impossible to imagine in ancient times. Not only did men always take precedence, but women alone were never called together for any public function. The "daughters of Jerusalem" must, therefore, have formed a special group. That that group was composed of the queens and concubines of the royal harem is indicated by at least four circumstances: (1) The summons was made on the day of Solomon's "wedding ceremony" (3:11d). This term, used only here, seems to be a collective, and, since there is no mention of a bride, it would appear to indicate the formal acceptance by the new King, at the beginning of his reign, of the harem he had inherited. Hence "Daughters of Jerusalem" becomes a sort of title, used to designate the royal queens and subordinate wives at that time and employed in specific application to a part of a larger body (namely, the women of the city in general), yet corresponding to the word "sons" as applied to the members of a guild, group, or class. (2) The group so designated manifests a proprietary interest in the royal house (5:9) that supports this view. (3) On the one occasion in the Song when women speak of the King among themselves, as individuals but at the same time collectively (1:2–4), the language they use is natural and appropriate only to members of a royal harem; on that occasion they are addressed as "Daughters of Jerusalem" (1:5). (4) A literal equating of the "Daughters" with the "queens and concubines" occurs in the synonymous parallelism in 6:9.

According to 6:8, there were one hundred and forty queens and concubines. This, with an indefinite number of servant girls, easily makes a total of three or four hundred persons summoned to meet the King on his arrival from some sort of journey. Since we are, therefore, assured of the presence of the harem and of the King, the setting can scarcely be other than Solomon's palace (1 Kings 7:2) in Jerusalem and we are clearly introduced to a royal-harem scene.

Solomon is thus definitely introduced at this point, and the words that follow, spoken to the girl, must be uttered by him unless the scene can be shown to have shifted. The maiden, too, if she is the object of the King's attention, must be present at the time in the palace, along with the harem, unless a change of scene can be established. Such a change of scene is precluded by the fact that the girl formally addresses her first speech in the Song to the "Daughters of Jerusalem" and then continues with a series of adjurations all directed at this group (2:7; 3:5; 5:8; 8:4). These oath formulas make it clear that up to and including the last one (8:4) she is in the presence of the ladies of the harem. That her speeches are not mere apostrophes, or directed to other persons in some other setting, is clear from the replies of this

8

group to the maiden, whom they always designate by the same epithet ("fairest among women"). Thus 1:8 is an immediate rejoinder to 1:5–7; 5:9 is their answer to 5:2–8; and 6:1 is evoked by 5:10–16.

Time and place settings consequently become explicit for the major part of the Song. Their establishment is correspondingly decisive in effecting a new concept of its literary form. The reason for this will appear presently. As the Song stands in the traditional arrangement, no such settings are required, and, superficially, it is by no means clear that they are defensible.

When an ancient literary work that has been transmitted for generations shows a lack of accord between inner requirements and outward form, it is reasonable to assume that the work has suffered a measure of conscious or unconscious manipulation. With that consideration we come to a third factor that may have influenced the form in which the Song has survived, namely, displacement and editorial rearrangement of certain elements. Such phenomena are not infrequent in other parts of the Old Testament: Pss. 9 and 10, for example, were originally one, as is demonstrated by the acrostic arrangement; Ps. 108 is made up of Ps. 57:7–11 and Ps. 60:5–12; and Ps. 19 appears to be an incomplete nature psalm (vss. 1–6) that was later filled out with a didactic poem on the Law (vss. 7–14). There is, accordingly, no a priori argument against similar changes having occurred in the Song, and they can hardly be denied if a more logical and normal arrangement is discernible, especially if adequate reasons for them are evident.

As the text of the Song stands in the present translation, the words that follow the announcement of Solomon's approach (see 3:6–11), namely, 4:1–6, are logically and naturally his first speech to the maiden (actually, he is represented as speaking to no one else), but in the traditional arrangement there are several other, earlier remarks made to the girl (1:9–11, 15; 2:2) which, in view of the presence of the harem, can be attributed only to the King. Furthermore, the entire section 1: 2—3: 5 starts without introduction and without indication of the setting; 1: 2–7, in particular, is completely without motivation, and the speakers are not identified. Since, however, the Daughters of Jerusalem are addressed in 1: 5, 2: 7, and 3: 5 and since it cannot be doubted that it is they who speak in 1: 8, we may be certain that we are dealing with a part of the harem scene, but one that is now disjointed and out of order, for not only Solomon but the Daughters of Jerusalem, too, are first introduced in 3: 6–11.

This, however, is not the only confusion in regard to the King's first speech (4: 1–6). No change of speaker or of person addressed is indicated at 4: 7, yet suddenly, without warning, the scene apparently shifts to the Lebanon Mountains; the spot is described as full of danger, and the girl is anxiously urged to flee. This setting and the attitude of the speaker mark a complete break with 4: 1–6, and it might well be concluded that what follows is entirely extraneous and independent were it not for the certain presence of the Daughters of Jerusalem in the web of the thought (cf. 5: 8–9). Furthermore, 5: 2 indicates that we are dealing with dream phenomena. These two circumstances are sufficient to show that the violent change of scene is only apparent. The dream factor does not, however, make it any easier to assign 4: 7 ff. to Solomon, and 4: 16 definitely eliminates that possibility.

The sequel to 4: 1–6 is obviously, therefore, not 4: 7 ff.; yet 4: 6 does demand a sequel. The language is highly figurative, but it clearly calls for some action by the King. In view of the reference to the person of the maiden in v. 5, all the requirements of the context would be satisfied if at this point the King sought to embrace her, and it would have been less than natural, under the circumstances, if the gesture had not included a kiss. The text, to be sure, is not explicit, but this may have been deliberate on the part of the poet, since it is not evident to what extent the

King succeeded in his intent, as will be noted later; yet, elsewhere, in verses which depict a similar situation and which can be
spoken logically only by the King (7: 7–9*a*), the act of embracing
and kissing is described in much detail.

This conception of the King's gesture would lead one to expect a discernible reaction from those present, the harem as well
as the girl. So far as the harem is concerned, we need a passage
containing an interchange of assertions by the women in regard
to the King's favors. The verses in 1: 2–4 are the only ones in
the Song that satisfy this condition. As the lines stand traditionally, however, they contain no antecedents for the pronouns and
give no hint of their relation to the rest of the poem; the passage
is suspended as if in a vacuum. But if the verses are placed directly after 4: 6, the pronouns refer unmistakably to the members
of the harem and the lines take on life and meaning in reference
to the context.

As has been remarked, the passage does not actually mention
the King's embrace of the maiden, but only on the assumption
that he tried to kiss her can 1: 2*a* be read with meaning in this
scene, that is, with the emphasis on *me* in both the singular and
the collective sense. Evidently the King had neither embraced
nor kissed any of the harem on this occasion. It was very natural
and right that they should desire such attentions, but what
prompted their common expression of that emotion at this point?
What elicited their eager protestations of a love and loyalty that
had been neither challenged nor sought? Why the added assertion that of course the servant girls are bound to love Solomon?
It seems evident from these declarations that the King had just
sought to kiss the girl in their presence (cf. 1: 2*ab*), and that she
recoiled from his advances, just as she very probably did at 7: 9*b*
(cf. v. 9*a*). The ladies of the harem, though doubtless secretly
pleased, naturally chose to express shock at her behavior and
self-righteously siezed the opportunity to affirm their own fervid
devotion.

Moreover, the girl's words, when she speaks a moment later, strengthen this impression. She says nothing to the King in either apology or explanation, but makes her remarks directly to the harem; indirectly, however, her words are a rejoinder to him as well as to the women. (This usurpation of the conversation by the women in the King's presence is a notable feature of the dialogues.) The King has stressed her beauty, and before she can say anything the women assert that of course the servant girls love Solomon, they cannot rightly do otherwise (1: 3, 4). At this point the maiden declares that, though comely, she is very dark, swarthy indeed; she mentions her complexion and her peasant origin as reasons why the harem and its lord should not regard her. And, in the eyes of the harem, she adds insult to injury by declaring her deep and soulful attachment to a country shepherd; she implies, further, that her present separation from him is compromising her character (1: 7). The women are quick to sense her meaning, and more than a hundred voices (6: 8) speak, as one, their amused scorn (1: 8). As for the King, her sentiments can hardly seem to him more than an expression of puppy love. Besides, the girl has as yet mentioned no lover by name. Then, too, is she not at the palace, that is, at his disposal (1: 6e), and hence as good as a member of the royal establishment already? He addresses her, accordingly, in the language of confident possession (1: 9), though he appeals to her vanity with the promise of jewelry (1: 11). And he maintains this attitude in the rest of his remarks in this context (1: 15; 2: 2), in spite of the fact that in her later speeches in this passage the girl not only names her lover (1: 13–14), but speaks of him in relation to their future home (1: 16–17).

The remainder of the passage up to 3: 6 is addressed by the maiden to the women, and ends with a repeated adjuration that they stir not up nor awaken love until it please (3: 5; cf. 2: 7). These admonitions refer to 1: 2–4, the lines in which the harem commended the love of the servant girls for Solomon. The maiden chides the women for this attitude and bids them let nature take its course in such matters. Even before her first oath of entreaty, however, it is evident that the situation in which she finds herself has roused in her a still deeper and more poignant love for the absent shepherd (2: 5–6).

As a result of these considerations it will be seen that if 3: 6—4: 6 is transferred to the beginning, the change knits together the entire context, gives the action a natural and logical sequence where it was previously lacking, and makes the harem scene virtually inescapable.

To the Judean editor, who had decided that the reading "my beloved" was only an epithet applied to Solomon, there could be no inherent objection to linking 4: 1–6 with 4: 7 ff.; on the contrary, there would be ample warrant for doing so if it seemed advantageous. He might with equal propriety have rearranged similarly anything in the song attributed to the "beloved" (2: 10–15 or 5: 2, for instance). The reference to Solomon that he saw (see p. 17) in 4: 16 was to him superlative evidence that all that preceded was uttered by the King.

The only question that requires consideration is, Why did the editor think his arrangement of the text so desirable that he made the changes involved? Three major reasons may be noted: (1) The passage beginning at 4: 7 contains the finest, loftiest, and most beautiful sentiments in praise of the maiden to be found in the Song. (2) It furnishes the one instance in which the girl acknowledges and accepts the words spoken in her praise and frankly reciprocates their sentiment. (3) It is the only passage that uses the word "bride" in addressing the maiden. In a word, if this passage expressed the attitude of both Solomon and the girl, there could be no question of their wholehearted acceptance of each other as bride and groom. And if that were assured, the honor and dignity of Solomon would be preserved. In comparison, nothing else in the poem mattered to the editor. As it was, he undoubtedly felt that without this arrangement the case for Solomon was by no means clear or convincing.

A number of circumstances account for this feeling on the part of the editor. To begin with, he was, *ex hypothesi*, fully aware of the harem scene with its Daughters-of-Jerusalem ensemble and its two principal characters, the King and the girl. He thus knew that at the outset she had declared her deep attachment for a country shepherd and that her separation from him had plunged her into the greatest distress (cf. 1:7). He knew, furthermore, that the women of the harem recognized this attachment, at first with mild disgust (cf. 1:8), then with open scorn (cf. 5:9), but, finally, charmed by her portrayal of the youth, with such sympathy that they sought to join her in searching for him (cf. 6:1). Moreover, although the editor consistently interprets the designation she uses for her lover as an epithet applied to Solomon, he nonetheless knew that both before and after 4:7—5:1 she had described him as a shepherd (cf. 1:7; 6:2, 3). He knew, too, that even after this passage the maiden had repeatedly expressed her pain at being separated from the one she loved and her desire to return to him and to her native village (5:2–8; 6:2–3; 7:11—8:3); in 5:8, indeed, she had urged the women in Solomon's presence that if they should find her lover they should tell him that she was sick with longing. Finally, in the concluding scene (8:5–14), in which it is clear that the lover is present throughout (vss. 6, 14), the girl does mention Solomon by name (vss. 11, 12)—for the first and only time in the Song—but in v. 11 she refers to him in the third person and the editor could hardly have failed to recognize that the King was, therefore, not present; nor could he have interpreted the direct address to Solomon in v. 12 as anything but an apostrophe.

The Judean editor thus had urgent reason for making it unmistakable that 4:7 ff. was spoken by the King, since, as the text

stood, that was by no means explicit or unequivocal. He indubitably believed that this could best be accomplished by joining
the utterances in 3: 6—4: 6 to those in 4: 7 ff. What if this
change did so disrupt the harem scene that it could no longer be
distinguished as a unit? That scene was troublesome anyway
from his standpoint, and, besides, its loss was nothing compared to
the gains he expected to derive from his own arrangement. Nor
was he disturbed by the possibility that this shifting of 3: 6—4: 6
would throw all that precedes, and indeed the entire poem, into
such chaos that no tenable theory of the Song as a whole could
thereafter ever be formulated on the basis of his rearrangement.

Even after this transposition there were still, from the editor's
viewpoint, many disturbing problems. Why, for example, was
the maiden never identified? Why should the great Solomon
have been concerned with such a nonentity? Why should the girl
have repeatedly urged the harem not to stir up love when she
herself seemed to be so deeply in love? Was she really as much
in love with a country shepherd as she said (1: 5–7) and as the
harem seemed to believe (1: 8)? After the events of Chapter 4
did the women still think it was that shepherd she was describing
in 5: 10–16, and was it he whom they wished to help her find
(6: 1)? If she had at first loved a shepherd, why, after accepting
Solomon, did she keep on describing her "beloved" as a shepherd? Why did she dream over and over of being separated
from her "beloved" and of being unable to join him when
Solomon had never been out of reach? Why did she, in the
presence of Solomon, express after Chapter 4 the same sense of
separation and the same longing for the embrace of the "beloved"
as she had earlier? Did Solomon go with her to her village home
and, if so, why is that fact not indicated? Why, instead, is his
name mentioned in this scene as if he were not present (8: 11)?
Finally, why should the Song reach its climax in an obscure
village, and the girl bring it to an end by telling her "beloved"

to go away, to go away, furthermore, not as a king, but as a wild stag of the hill country? If the editor's rearrangement had the effect of obscuring some of these troublesome queries, or at least of breaking their cumulative force—as it undoubtedly did—he must surely have regarded this in itself as a special argument in its favor. The complete confusion that resulted was the enormous price he was willing to pay in the attempt to make Solomon appear the great lover and the true bridegroom.

Incidentally, there may be at this point a minor change in the text due to the Judean editor. As is indicated by the maiden in 4: 16, the passage 4: 7–15 is actually the utterance of the lover. But 4: 7 ff. is exceedingly abrupt, from any standpoint. In the other places where the lover is introduced reminiscently the fact is indicated by the words "The voice of 'my beloved'" (see 2: 8; 5: 2); without this indication in the text these transitions would be equally abrupt and obscure. It will be noted that in 2: 8 the expression directly follows the admonition to the women (v. 7). According to our thesis, 4: 7 originally followed the same exhortation in 3: 5. If 4: 7 in the original began with the line "The voice of 'my beloved'" the circumstance would doubtless have made his rearrangement seem even more reasonable to the editor. But if that were the situation, the phrase would be worse than superfluous once 4: 6 and 4: 7 ff. were juxtaposed, for it would interrupt rather than help the flow of the King's words. We may be sure, accordingly, that, if present, the phrase would certainly have been eliminated. In the original, however, it would have been as valid and as functionally useful as it is in the places where we now find it in the text.

A fourth clue to the original of the Song may be discovered through a close scrutiny of the pointed text. Wherever that text requires an otherwise unknown meaning for a form and the unpointed text would yield a known word and a recognized usage, the more normal Hebrew of the unpointed text has a legitimate claim to preference, especially if there is good reason to suspect special interest in the pointing on the part of the editor. There are three words in the Song to which this suggestion is applicable.

The first word, *d o d,* twice repeated in 5: 9 and variously rendered "beloved," "lover," or "darling," requires an anomalous meaning for an otherwise normal word. As is well known, the word *d o d* in Hebrew signifies "uncle," which is clearly impossible in the context. The unpointed text, however, furnishes the consonantal basis for one of the most familiar and famous proper names in the Scriptures, that is, "David," which is written almost exclusively in this form in the earlier books. Furthermore, as will be shown, not only is "David" a legitimate reading, but it changes the lines in which it occurs from meaningless combinations of words to significant parts of the thought structure.

The second word, *d o d i,* is commonly rendered "my beloved," and this, also, is an anomalous meaning for a normal Hebrew form. As already noted, the word *d o d* means "uncle"; *d o d i* should, then, be "my uncle," but this is not possible in the context. At the same time, the meaning "lover" or "beloved" is conveyed in Hebrew by quite another word, *y a d î d .* In view of the context, therefore, we are warranted in disregarding the pointing here. A reading that satisfies all the requirements is *D o d a i ,* which is a known early Hebrew name— that of the grandfather of one of David's heroes (cf. 2 Sam. 23: 9), for example. Compounds from this root are recognized as ancient and early became obsolete,[13] but they exemplify a type of formation that appears widely. The use of the word as a personal name is no modern innovation, for it appears throughout the Syriac version of the Song, which transliterates, but never attempts to translate, the form. The Syriac thus preserves the shepherd lover as a distinct character, together with the attendant implications for the story.

[13] See G. B. Gray, *Hebrew Proper Names* (London, 1896), p. 63.

The third word whose pointing is questionable is variously translated in both ancient and modern versions as "my love," "my friend," or "my dear." The Hebrew form *ra'yathi* in the Masoretic text is assumed to be the feminine of *re'eh*, meaning "friend," "companion," plus the pronominal suffix for "my." But the Masoretic reading is not the feminine of the word for "friend," for no such word for "friend" is known. The possibility that this consonantal pattern occurs in the Kethib of Jd. 11: 37 is rendered doubtful by the presence of the same word in the next verse written with normal waw rather than yodh; hence the yodh in v. 37 may be only a copyist's error. But even if the yodh were original the normal reading would be a feminine participial form with internal yodh: *ro'iyyoth*.[14] There is thus no linguistic precedent or pattern for our Masoretic form. A normal pointing in the Song would yield *ro'iyyathi*, i.e. a feminine participle of a lamedh hē verb with internal yodh, plus a final yodh. Morphologically the form could be referred to the root *ra'ah*, "to associate with," and hence could be translated "friend"; or it might be derived from the same root, which also has the meaning "to feed," and so have the meaning "shepherdess." But according to literary usage, though we have *re'eh* (feminine *re'ah*), "friend," there seems to be no corresponding use of the participle from this root; whereas from *ra'ah* meaning "to feed" we have *ro'ah*, "shepherdess" or "shepherd girl" (feminine participle; cf. Gen. 29: 9), which is directly equivalent to *ro'iyyathi*. It is much more probable, therefore, that in the original the root meaning would be "to feed." The yodh ending could be either the first person pronominal suffix "my," or ḥireq *campaginis*, which occurs only when attached to a participle to give it distinction.[15] Since the form with final yodh is used whenever the girl is addressed (except by the women), it is clear

---

[14] Cf. Gesenius–Kautzsch, *Hebrew Grammar* (Oxford, 1910), 75v.
[15] Cf. Gesenius–Kautzsch, *op. cit.*, 90m.

that the term is applied as an epithet, but whether the speaker in each instance added the suffix as an expression of personal relationship, or whether this is the ḥireq *campaginis,* is not immediately apparent. Does the narrative give us any clue on this point? One evidence that the ending is not the pronominal suffix is found when the lover uses the epithet and, in the same passage, refers to the girl as "bride" but does not feel sure enough of the situation to say "my bride" (cf. textual note 75). In that context (4: 7 ff.) he could scarcely have meant "my shepherdess." This evidence is corroborated by the fact that the word to which the final yodh is attached is used as an epithet by more than one person and that it is a participle, which, as we have noted, is the one grammatical form to which the ending is added as a simple mark of distinction.

The epithet "shepherdess" or "shepherd girl" comports well with the humble rural origin the maiden claims (cf. 1: 5–6), with her intimate knowledge of shepherd life, with her steadfast devotion to a shepherd lover, and with her apparent position as a servant girl in the royal harem (cf. textual notes 33 and 62). The rendering "my friend" or "my love" follows the lead of the Judean editor in attempting to dignify the King's relation to the girl, and is part of his failure to realize that she was a servant who was being reassured by the new King that she was still wanted in the palace.

Here, then, is an epithet that was used in what amounted to the inner family circle, and the Song had no occasion for anything else. Even so, it is worth remark that the girl's real name, the name by which she was known when she was first discovered by the agents of King David, does not appear in either the Song or the book of Kings. In the Song the term that comes closest to identifying her is "Shunammite" (6:13), but this only indicates her native village; it does nothing to relate her to a particular family, which was the minimum requirement in such case.

In the book of Kings, where definite identification is assumed and should, therefore, be present, the omission may be purely accidental.   To be sure, the girl is referred to in Kings as "Abishag," but this name by itself is even less distinctive than "Shunammite," so far as family relationship is concerned.   It may be said that the simplest and most usual way of identifying an unmarried daughter was by means of the expression *b a th*, that is, "daughter of so-and-so," in conjunction with the father's name.   (This method was so general that some very famous women of the Bible are known to us by no other type of designation—e.g. the daughter of Pharaoh who adopted Moses and the daughter of Jephthah [Jd. 11: 37]).   That being so, it may be that "Abishag" was the name of the girl's father and that the element *b a th* at one time appeared with it, but later inadvertently dropped out. This could easily have happened if, where "Abishag" first occurs (1 Kings 1: 3), the form *b a th* had been blurred and consequently misread as *'e th* (the sign of the direct object), that is, if there had been a mistake of a single consonant (cf. Hosea 8: 6).   It will be noted in each of the four verses where the girl is subsequently referred to (1: 15; 2: 17, 21, 22) that both "Abishag" and "Shunammite" are used, as they are here.   If *b a th* did at one time occur in this first instance, either term alone would have been quite sufficient afterward, and "Shunammite" would have been more natural under the circumstances.   But once *b a th* had been lost, a later annotator might well have felt that all known designations should be employed, since all were at best defective; so he might have added "Abishag," which he found in 1 Kings 1: 3, to "Shunammite" in each of the other references.

The reasoning of the editor of the Song is seen to be clear and straightforward.   His first, major premise was that Solomon was honored in the poem.   Any other possibility was to him unthinkable.   To have admitted that the epithet for the lover was a proper name or that it designated anyone but Solomon would have ruined the poem from his standpoint. But once the correct sequence is restored it becomes apparent that the lover is not Solomon, regardless of whether the epithet is a proper name or not. Rearrangement of the text enabled the editor to sidestep that conclusion. Furthermore, though he doubtless knew of many proper names ending in yodh, he also knew that a final yodh could indicate the first person pronominal suffix "my." If, therefore, Solomon addressed the girl by a term ending in yodh, it would seem natural to the editor to take it as "my," that is, as an expression of the King's acceptance of her (i.e. "my friend," and so on). Similarly, when the girl spoke of her lover and used a form ending in yodh, he again took the ending to mean "my" and to indicate her acceptance of the person she had in mind; and he assumed that that person was the King. Finally, since he had already given a new value to the epithet employed by the girl, it is only logical that when he met the same consonantal form without what he regarded as the suffix he should consider it to be the same word. It is evident, however, that once he had come to this last conclusion he could do nothing with the lines in which the word without the final yodh occurs pointed in this fashion (cf. 5:9); nor has anyone else who has used this reading done any better.

In summary, the restoration of the harem scene and the result-ant emergence of the shepherd lover as a separate person decidedly alter our interpretation of everything attributed to the heroine, and this cannot but vitally affect our concept of the deeper thought structure of the Song. The consequent recovery of the words to be ascribed to the lover clarifies and delimits the words and sentiments of the King. It will be noted that in this process the tradition of Solomon as the true suitor, the great lover, of the Song is shown to be completely beside the mark. There is no courtship; the girl is at the palace, among the women of the harem, from the beginning. The King makes no request of her and invites her to nothing. His speeches, therefore, viewed as a unit, consist only of acknowledgment of a newly acquired member of the harem and physical appraisal of her in terms of desirable property. This estimate of Solomon's part in the Song agrees well with the evidence derived from the late gloss (1: 1) that the characterization of him in the poem was original, but Northern in source. As will be noted in detail (see pp. 31–39), the poet actually used these essential facts, dramatically and purposely, to the disadvantage of Solomon.

The transfer of 3: 6—4: 6 to the beginning has the surprising effect that it throws the entire Song into two definite and coordinate scenes, both introduced by the same expression: "Who [or 'what'] is that coming up from the wilderness." In the first we see the litter of Solomon approaching Jerusalem and hear the summons to the women of the royal household to go forth and greet the King. This evolves into a royal-palace scene that continues through 8: 4, as is clear from the series of speeches addressed to the ladies of the harem by the girl, and their replies. Here the second scene begins, and the girl is seen, accompanied by her lover, approaching her native village and her mother's home. The setting of this scene is made continuous and concrete by the presence of her brothers, to whom she recalls an earlier conversation.

Outwardly the two parts present the sharpest contrast, for in one the setting is the royal palace in Jerusalem and in the other it is a simple peasant village. Inwardly they have organic unity due to the presence of the same central figure, the girl, and to the continuity of the theme throughout. In the first scene the emphasis is on the maiden's preoccupation with her absent lover, on her deep attachment to him, her loyalty, and her conviction that her love is returned, and on her passionate longing to rejoin him. In the second scene we see that desire realized, for she appears in the company of her lover and the main dialogue records the triumph of their mutual devotion. It is clear, consequently, that the poem has true internal unity and requires no additions or subtractions to that end. This unity of form and content, which becomes apparent essentially by means of a single rearrangement of material, makes it evident that the pointed text is rightly to be regarded as equivalent to a distinct recension of the original.

HISTORICAL COHERENCE OF THE SONG

Our preliminary study of the Song's literary form has resulted in its articulation as an organic whole in a historical setting. The validity of that thesis remains to be examined.

One test of the poem's unity will be its consistency with a general point of view, and that consistency will naturally be related to the age and place of origin of the work, in so far as these can be determined. The general question of its age and origin has been provisionally answered by the tentative assumption of a Northern source, at least for its central nucleus. The unity we have ascribed to the poem makes this view more convincing, indeed almost mandatory, since a song about Solomon written in the South could scarcely begin with a scene at the royal palace in Jerusalem and have its climax in a rustic Northern village, with no other participants than peasants clearly indicated in that final scene.

A second test of the Song's unity is the extent to which it coincides with historical tradition. Its specific dating is dependent on the degree to which the materials can be tested against extant accounts of the kingdom from the days of Solomon to the fall of North Israel. The concept formulated here in regard to the work would lead one to expect in it allusions that would fit into or enlarge our knowledge of certain traditions current at the time of its writing and associated with events it presupposes but so well known to the author's contemporaries as not to require extended statement. A number of such allusions can be discerned.

It was an unquestioned belief of the time that Solomon's mother Bathsheba was largely responsible for the rise to the throne of this, one of the youngest of David's sons (1 Kings 1), but the book of Kings, which preserves the story, makes no mention of a crown or a coronation. The Song, on the other hand, takes the tradition of Solomon's rise for granted and assumes that his mother is too notorious (perhaps because of her association with the acts of adultery and murder committed by David) to require naming, but it speaks of a crown, and says it was Solomon's mother who accomplished his coronation (3:11). There is no reason to doubt the truth of this detail in the Song, and its omission in Kings may well have been due to the unsavory reputation of the queen mother; the compiler may have felt that this investiture at her hands could not contribute to the glory of Solomon and so have deliberately left it out.

Furthermore, it has hitherto been assumed that the heroine of the Song was unidentified, except once, when she was called the "Shunammite" (6:13 [LXX]). Is it possible that this was all that was required? In other words, had the author grounds to suppose that she was such a well-known personage that this one epithet was, in the particular story, sufficient to distinguish her?

It will be recalled that in the account of David's last days there is the story of the selection of a beautiful maiden from the village of Shunem in North Israel to act as his nurse. It is explicitly stated, however, that the King had no conjugal relations with her, and thus her attendance on him did not officially make her a member of the harem (1 Kings 1:1-4). This is confirmed by Adonijah's request of Bathsheba that the girl be given to him in marriage (1 Kings 2:17).

24

The narrative in Kings relates that the maiden was chosen and brought to Jerusalem because of her exceptional beauty (1 Kings 1:3–4); the Song assumes that these facts are well known and simply refers to the girl by the epithet "Shunammite" and by the phrase, in the mouths of the ladies of the harem, "fairest among women."   But Kings gives no hint of how the choice was made or of who made it, whereas the Song sheds light on both these points.   A brief scene of reminiscence in the Song recalls the praises uttered by certain of the royal ladies when they first caught sight of the girl (6:9d–10) by the side of the great trunk road that ran through the valley of Jezreel, passing well within range of the village of Shunem. The maiden explains in this scene how she happened to be there: It was a day in early spring, and she had gone down from her home on the higher slopes to a nut orchard in the valley to see the promise of bud and blossom (6:11).   There she noted on the road an unwonted procession of chariots, and her curiosity got the better of her.   Before she was aware she found herself among them (6:12).   It was then that the queens and concubines saw her and exclaimed over her beauty (6:10). But her first impulse when she realized that she had attracted their attention was to flee, and only their repeated entreaties, "Stay, stay" (6:13), brought her back to them.   The scene gives the clear impression that this was the occasion that led to her being chosen as David's nurse (cf. 6:9–10).

It seems probable, therefore, that no matter who else was out searching for the most beautiful maiden in all Israel, certain members of the royal harem made the choice.   This is reasonable, for, since the girl would take precedence of the entire harem in caring for the aged King, the royal ladies could not fail to be intensely interested in the selection; Bathsheba, the mother of Solomon, may well have been one of them.   In addition, the very fact that on this occasion some of their number were so far from home, with no other apparent reason, strongly suggests that they may have been formally entrusted with the choice.

Thus, while neither the book of Kings nor the Song gives the whole picture, the fact that they supplement each other in this fashion shows that they are dealing with the same situation; the story gains in clarity and in completeness. Since it was well known that a nation-wide search had been made for the most beautiful girl in the land, the Song could refer to the occasion when she was first discovered with such a minimum of detail as to seem enigmatic until brought into focus with 1 Kings 1:3, and could at the same time add certain essential bits of information to that account.

It becomes obvious from these considerations why the Song could assume that the presence of a Shunammite peasant girl at the royal palace (which is now apparent in the harem scene) would be taken for granted by a contemporary audience and, though a matter of importance, would require no explanation; it is likewise obvious why the Song could assume common knowledge of how the girl could be at the palace but not a member of the harem. It also becomes clear why the phrase "fairest among women" was sufficient as a designation so far as the harem was concerned, since certain of its members had probably been instrumental in her selection on the basis of superlative beauty.

The reason for Solomon's paying particular attention to the maiden on the day of his "wedding" to the queens and concubines (3:11) is similarly obscure until his action is related to the situation described in 1 Kings 1. Then it is seen that he singles her out, praises her beauty, promises her jewelry, offers his caresses, and reminds her of the occasion on which she first came to the notice of the court in order to assure her that she is now to be accepted and approved as a bona fide member of the royal establishment. And clearly this was the moment for such assurance if it was to be effective.

According to the law in ancient Israel, a woman could not protect her person from her employer, and hence she could not serve in a household without becoming potentially the wife of the head of the house (cf. Ex. 21:7–8). Such would have been the status of the Shunammite had it not been for the condition of the aged King David. And if nothing else had been involved, the new King might, without further ceremony, have inherited her as a member of his harem simply by virtue of her presence in what was now his household. But, as has been noted, Adonijah, Solomon's brother, asked for her in marriage, and after that her status could no longer be safely left in doubt. To be sure, Adonijah was speedily executed, but other adventurers might wish to make capital of her closeness to David, as he had probably intended to do. The significance that Solomon attached to the girl at this time is evident in his remarks in 1 Kings 2:22.

It will be noted in the Song that Solomon never offers the maiden any alternative. It is assumed that the King's favor is an advancement and an honor that no one of her position could refuse. Solomon's attitude and actions in regard to her are seen to be a part of the political situation of the time, a feature of domestic state policy motivated by the girl's importance because of her association with David.

The Song takes for granted that it will be understood that Solomon was already acquainted with the girl. The narrative in Kings states the specific conditions that make this certain. As the nurse of David she was obliged to live and move within the innermost circle of the royal family for some time (cf. 1 Kings 1:15), and Bathsheba and her son Solomon were at the heart of that circle (cf. 1 Kings 1:11–27). There the maiden

27

must have been almost as well known as she was in her village home.

As has already been indicated, the reference to Lebanon (4:8) appears to be utterly disconnected from the context. But it should be noted that the language here is highly figurative, for, whereas Hebrew is extremely sensitive to the ups and downs of topography, the present passage, which recites the names of the highest mountains of the region, expresses no awareness of varying altitudes. The "Lebanon" of this section proves to be only a symbol used by the speaker for a spot he thinks full of danger for the maiden. Furthermore, it is apparently the very place where the girl is at the moment, and the context shows that she is still in the presence of the harem, the "Daughters of Jerusalem" (5:8); in other words, she is still in the palace of Solomon. Now we learn from Kings that Solomon's palace was famed throughout the land as the "House of the Forest of Lebanon" (cf. 1 Kings 7:2) because, owing to the slope of the hill on which it stood, it rested at least in part upon a basement or crypt in which were three rows of pillars, forty-five in all, made of the trunks of cedars of Lebanon. Since the harem scene in the royal palace was explicit in the original Song, no contemporary Israelite could have misunderstood the reference to Lebanon, and, with it, the reflection of a North Israelite concept of Solomon's domestic establishment (4:8). But it no doubt puzzled the Judean editor later on, for it must have been impossible for him to picture Solomon's magnificent palace in any such terms. However, in view of his various assumptions in regard to the text and his free editing of it, this could have been for him only one of several equally dark enigmas.

The fact that the term "bride" occurs five times in 4:9—5:1, always in the absolute, has been hitherto inexplicable. Why did the writer use it consistently without a suffix? Why did he use it only in this section? And how could he adopt this form of

reference so abruptly and expect to be understood? The lines
4: 7—5: 1 contain the account of a dream experience on the part
of the maiden (cf. 5: 2). In this passage two things are significant. First, the lover (cf. 4: 16) is represented as using the
word "bride" in apposition to the word "sister," but as always
saying "my sister" and never "my bride." Second, the pleas
to the maiden to flee from "Lebanon" (the palace) express, in
her dream, a sense of fear and personal danger that does not
occur elsewhere in the Song. Why should this sense of fear have
been so closely connected with the term "bride"? Is there anything in the circumstances surrounding the maiden that could
serve as its basis in this association?   498 6

When we turn to Kings we find that Adonijah's request for
permission to make the Shunammite his wife (see 1 Kings 2: 17),
though now probably somewhat out of order,[16] without doubt
preceded the events depicted in the Song. There is no indication
that prior to that request there was anything to disturb the
maiden's sense of security or any threat to the prospect that
she would ultimately be allowed to return home if she desired.
Afterward, however, all was changed. To be sure, she did not
become Adonijah's bride, for he was quickly eliminated, but
the fact that a prince had asked for her hand must have made
it evident to her that she had become a political pawn of such
importance that her withdrawal from the palace would be extremely difficult. It could be expected that whoever came to
the throne would plan to include her, for reasons of state, as
a member of the harem. Henceforth, in terms of her loyalty
to her shepherd lover, the palace was a very dangerous place
for her to be. The origin of the fear motif is thus clear. Yet,
since the word "bride" indicated only a potential state and one

[16] Leroy Waterman, "Some Historical and Literary Consequences of Probable
Displacement in 1 Kings 1–2," *Journal of the American Oriental Society*, 60
(1940): 383–390.

that was not yet realized in the poem, the lover could still be thought of as pressing his suit, and the girl dreamed that he did so, in language as exalted and beautiful as was ever meant for woman's ear; her own response is so wholehearted that there can be no question but what the lovers are inwardly secure.

The lover woos the maiden, in the dream, by the expression of lofty and beautiful sentiment and also by his adroit use of the two terms "sister" and "bride." In the West a lover cannot say "my sister" and "my bride" of the same person, but in the polygamous East, where a man might marry his stepsister, this was possible (cf. Gen. 20:12). Yet at this point in the Song, though the lover could use the endearment "my sister," he could not say "my bride," or feel sure of ever being able to say it so long as she remained in the palace after the Adonijah episode. He could, however, use the absolute form "bride" both as an ominous warning of what might lie ahead of her at the palace and as a veiled reminder of his own doubtful prospects. In other words, the term is a concentrated expression of the girl's dilemma: she foresees that she must soon become a bride, but whose bride is still open to question.

It must be supposed then that Solomon's approach to the girl was no surprise to her. Her fear had been excited by Adonijah's action, which could scarcely have remained unknown to her in the palace. She had sensed its implications for her own status and future, and she had been troubled by what her absent lover might think when he learned of her new "bride" prospect. When, therefore, her apprehensions were realized and she had to defend her attitude toward Solomon to King and harem, the recital of her dream (4:7 ff.) became one of her strongest weapons, for it showed, subtly but unmistakably, that the prospect that resulted from Adonijah's request had only filled her with anxiety and dread and that, far from turning her from her shepherd lover, it had strengthened and sealed that attachment.

Adonijah's request became common knowledge in Israel, and the events connected with it must have happened only a few days, at most, before those depicted in the harem scene (see pp. 29–30). Consequently, the term "bride" without the possessive "my" was all that was necessary, in view of the general awareness of the dangerous position of the maiden, to make the situation full appreciated. Once again the Song is seen to be dealing with an actual event, and again it adds to what we know from other sources. The book of kings was not interested in the maiden's attitude to Adonijah, but this dream sequence in the Song reflects her feeling in regard to him, and the representation is probably accurate, for if she resisted Solomon, she no doubt resented Adonijah as well.

We have pointed out that both Kings and the Song place the girl at the royal palace, but, that being so, how could the author of the Song nonchalantly assume the possibility of her release and return to her native village? It will be noted that, though the book of Kings starts out as if to give a prominent place to the Shunammite and though her importance is sustained until 2: 22, she totally disappears from the narrative thereafter. Why did the editor of Kings so suddenly lose all interest in her? It will be observed that he gives no indication that the maiden ever became a member of Solomon's harem, although his estimate of her (cf. 1 Kings 2: 22) shows that she had a good prospect of doing so. This evaluation, along with her prominent introduction, is all the more reason for expecting that if she did become the bride of Solomon the fact would be recorded. Absence of such a record is good evidence that the marriage did not take place.

Thus the book of Kings and the Song are at one in assuming that the girl did not enter the harem. There the interest of

Kings ends. The compiler was not further concerned with her fate; if he knew the reason for her withdrawal from the palace he did not record it, for it would have seemed derogatory to Solomon. The Song, on the other hand, picks up where Kings leaves off, and shows why the maiden did not join the harem and how her consequent release could be brought about without unduly affronting the King.

The problem that resulted from the Adonijah incident related in Kings was a simple but very real one: it was necessary to make sure that no aspirant to the throne would be able, through marriage, to use the prestige of the girl for political purposes. If she had been married, or even securely betrothed, no problem need have arisen. It is the art of the poem to show that she was betrothed (though the term is never used) to one of her own rank (2:16; 3:4; 4:16; 5:1; 6:3; 7:10) and so irrevocably that nothing could break the bond. And this was tactfully accomplished, not by a direct statement to Solomon himself, but by the girl's appeal to the assembled harem, in which she first states her case (1:5–7) and then meets their ridicule (1:8) with such a compelling description of her lover (2:8—3:5; 4:7—5:8) as to challenge their complacency (5:9), arouse their interest (5:10–16), and, finally, gain their open approval (6:1). Solomon is represented as having scant respect for the harem (2:2; 6:8–9), but he had no reason to doubt the verdict expressed in their reaction (6:1). However, a king with a vast harem could hardly be expected to have any serious regard for peasant love, and so he makes one further attempt to win the girl (6:4–10; 7:6–9a), which ends in his final rebuff (7:9b–10).

So the maiden in this fashion fully revealed the genuineness of her feeling for the shepherd and simultaneously accounted for her rejection of the King's favors. To be sure, she openly risked Solomon's displeasure as a consequence, but that did not cause her to flinch or waver. Love of her own choosing proved to be "strong as death" (cf. 8:6). In view of the bond she maintained with such firmness, there was, then, no reason for keeping her at the palace and good reason for her release, since the King's interest was a matter of political security rather than personal preference (cf. 6:8 and 1 Kings 11:3). The Song thus corroborates the tradition preserved in Kings and supplements the picture given there with certain essential details.

Within the general situation depicted by the Song, there is one passage whose writing calls for definite time limits. The natural force of 6:4ab ("You are beautiful, shepherd girl, as Tirzah, comely as Jerusalem") has never been successfully denied. The parallel is with Jerusalem, and the important thing is that Tirzah comes first. The attempt to reduce Tirzah to an abstract noun doubly misses the mark, for only a place name meets the requirements. But it is unthinkable that the historical Solomon could ever have made the comparison. In his mouth the verse is pure invention, for it could have been applicable only after North Israel had won its independence from Judah and while Tirzah was its capital, that is, from approximately 925 to 870 B.C.[17] Before 931 Tirzah was nothing but an obscure village, and after 870 Samaria was the single Northern city that could compare with Jerusalem. But the order of the comparison is such as would never have occurred to a Southern king or writer. The verse is basic evidence, therefore, not only of the Song's Northern origin, but of the date, within limits, of its writing, once its unity is conceded. We know that the struggle of North Israel for independence went on for over a generation and that war with Judah continued for years afterward (cf.

[17] See E. R. Thiele, "The Chronology of the Kings of Judah and Israel," *Journal of Near Eastern Studies*, 3 (1944): 148; and cf. W. F. Albright, "The Chronology of the Divided Monarchy of Israel," *Bulletin of the American Schools of Oriental Research*, 100 (1945): 16–22.

1 Kings 15: 6–7, 32). So long, then, as Tirzah served as the capital, it would have been difficult to find a more effective symbol of Israel's triumph than this comparison placed in the mouth of Solomon.

In the preceding discussion of the Song's historicity we have endeavored to show that the elements in the poem which confirm, supplement, or extend traditions preserved in Kings are sufficient to establish that the work as a unit deals with an actual episode at the beginning of Solomon's reign and that the episode was put into literary form in the North in the early days of the Divided Kingdom. From this we should expect that the Song would present an earlier and more original tradition in regard to certain details than appears in Kings, whose main redaction was probably exilic. That it does so is clear when we note the rather moderate-sized harem in the Song (6: 8) as compared with that in Kings (1 Kings 11: 3), as well as Solomon's modest bodyguard of sixty footmen (3: 7) in comparison with the fourteen hundred chariots and twelve thousand horsemen stationed in his chariot cities and *with the king* in Jerusalem (1 Kings 10: 26).

MOTIVATION

It remains to consider the motivation of the Song. What could have led to the writing of such a poem, and what did it signify to the age that produced it? We have, to begin with, the story of the Northern country girl who, because of her beauty, achieved a prestige and a renown memorable in both the North and the South. Was she not brought to Jerusalem to minister to Israel's first great king during his last days, and, while still there, had she not been sought in marriage by a prince who might eventually have made her queen of all Israel? But that story naturally faded from men's minds during the spectacular reign of Solomon, with whose rule her name was not linked

34

in popular tradition, and in the South, for some hitherto un-explained reason, no record survived of her later fate.

Solomon brought grinding poverty and the threat of revolt to the North, however, and, upon his death, North Israel broke away, the kingdom fell apart, and bitter civil strife ensued for more than a generation, till the separation was stabilized and North Israel established as an independent state. The strenuous period that followed Solomon's reign was one in which patriotism came to white heat in the North, and emphasis on things Israelitish rather than Judean received tremendous impetus. The period furnished an excellent atmosphere for a revival of interest in Israel's most beautiful maiden and in her fate after the hated Solomon came to the throne. In the North the story's sequel was known. There it was told that the girl had long been betrothed to a peasant youth from her native village and that, because of this attachment, she had resisted the allurements of the capital and the offers of the King; she had remained true to her shepherd and by her steadfastness in maintaining her love she had managed to gain her freedom and rejoin her betrothed in the North. Such are the basic facts preserved in the Song.

Had Solomon proved a kind and beneficent ruler, popular interest in the fair maid of Shunem might well have been as ephemeral in the North as is the attention usually bestowed on the winners of modern beauty contests. But the harrowing experiences of his reign and the strain of a long civil war against the tyranny of the South gave the story new meaning and new implications. The events of the girl's life and her struggle for freedom struck an answering chord in the consciousness of the nation. She was a North Israelite and, like Israel, had willingly served King David. On coming to the throne, Solomon sought to claim her, mainly for political reasons, but a deeper love, more compelling than any outward pomp and splendor, bound her to her humble Northern home and the friend of her childhood (cf. 8: 5). Alone and single-handed she fought to free herself from the power of Jerusalem's king and won her liberty because her love and loyalty were to the North and were stronger than death (see 8: 6).

Here were motives and values that could thrill every patriotic Israelite of the times. The romantic story, its Northern focus, and contemporary political conditions combined to enable a great writer to produce the finest lyric poetry in the language. In order to exalt and glorify the rural North in contrast to the artificial splendor of Solomon's court the author has given us the loveliest description of nature in springtime to be found in the Scriptures. By high-lighting certain features he placed love between man and woman on a plane hardly surpassed in literature. Moreover, the national setting enabled him to demonstrate the extravagance and the sensuality of Solomon. Note, for example, his royal litter appearing in clouds of dust yet perfumed with myrrh and frankincense (see 3: 6), his mare hitched to a chariot of Pharaoh (cf. 1: 9), his promise of gold and silver jewelry (cf. 1: 11), his description of the maiden, culminating in his attempted liberties with her person (see 7: 6–9a). More especially, Solomon the voluptuary gave the poet opportunity to picture him, in the presence of the assembled sixty queens, eighty concubines, and countless servant girls, as giving his undivided attention to the humble Northern peasant maid.

Since the girl had been selected and brought to Jerusalem because of her beauty the King could do no less than admit it, and he repeats the admission five times in sixteen verses. He then appraises her beauty in detail, beginning with her eyes and proceeding to her hair, teeth, lips, mouth, temples, neck and bosom (see 4: 1–5). The compliments on her hair, teeth, and temples he reiterates verbatim (see 6: 5–7). Once he likens her to his favorite mare hitched to the royal chariot; once he declares her as beautiful as either of the capital cities of the Divided Kingdom; once he says that in comparison with the ladies of the harem, she is a lily among brambles. Apart from the hint that the fine jewelry he promises her will improve her looks, this comprises his accounting of her beauty.

We know that, as a Northerner, the writer could have had neither love nor respect for Solomon, nor did he regard him as the true lover of the story. We know, rather, that both he and his fellow countrymen had good reason to hate and despise Israel's most magnificent king. To what end, then, were these compliments placed in the mouth of Solomon, and what can be discovered from the language in which they were phrased when they are viewed in the light of this attitude? The purpose is perfectly clear in 6: 4*ab*, where the girl's beauty is introduced only in order to give the Northern capital, Tirzah, precedence over Jerusalem; and the comparison is made all the more effective by being placed in the mouth of Solomon, although the writer thereby causes the King to speak in a manner entirely impossible for him as a historical person. We may conclude that the author would not hesitate to attribute to Solomon any language that suited his ends and his audience, regardless of historical fact or the King's dignity.

The simile of ewes herded together, when applied to the girl's teeth (4: 2), has a very particular connotation, whatever its artistic merits or demerits. Literally, not one tooth is lacking. It goes without saying that such an observation, no matter how expressed, is no remark for a suitor to make to a young woman who is his prospective bride. It is, however, precisely the type of comment that the prospective purchaser of a valuable domestic animal might normally and naturally utter, and indicates that the writer has cast Solomon in just that rôle. Moreover, such a comment in regard to an animal does not result from a casual glance; it ordinarily requires opening the mouth of the animal and making an accurate inspection of both the upper and the lower jaws. Although the result in this instance is declared to be eminently satisfactorily, the writer, as if to make the picture doubly clear, causes Solomon to repeat the observation (see 6: 6). The force of such a figure of speech could scarcely have been lost upon the prevailingly rural population of North Israel, whose wealth to a large extent consisted of domestic animals. With little doubt it pleasantly stimulated their derogatory opinion of Solomon.

The seriousness of some of the other similes is likewise suspect. The comparison of the girl's hair with a flock of goats (4: 1de) is lacking in clearness because of the uncertainty as to the meaning of the rare verb that is used, but if our suggestion in regard to this verb is valid (see textual note 19), the figure is anything but complimentary. The comparison with the mare (1: 9) is one that was rich in associations, but when the figure is extended to a mare hitched to the King's state chariot, it is evident that Solomon is represented as thinking primarily in terms of property. That the girl's neck is like an armed fortress capable of storing the shields of a thousand warriors is a plainly ludicrous image, and the author's contemporaries could scarcely have had any other impression of it.

The other comparisons are either too brief or too uncertain in their exact bearing to furnish any sure basis for evaluating them, but these examples are sufficient to show the character of the author's treatment of Solomon, and his method. No attempt to put Solomon in a favorable light in the Song can escape incongruity once these speeches are seen from the viewpoint of their original audience. Nor is it possible to construe them as infelicities in the author's style. His other figures are too superb for that, and the intent of the language is too evident.

The first requirement of the Song was the humiliation of Solomon, which was accomplished in the rebuff administered by a humble peasant girl from the North. Any supplementary details that contributed to his detraction were admissible, since, all together, they could never come up to the evils of his reign. The principal theme was the struggle of the servant girl for liberty and the love and loyalty through which she achieved it, and to the poet this theme was a symbol of the national hope for freedom from oppression. He voiced the plight of his people in the words of the maiden: "Alas, my own vineyard have I not kept," and he pointed to the goal and inspired them to a new zeal with her final exultant declaration: "My vineyard, my very own, is for myself."

The Song of Songs

1: 1   *The Song of Songs, which deals with Solomon.*[1]

PART I

HAREM SCENE AT THE ROYAL PALACE IN JERUSALEM[2]
(1: 2—8: 4)

SOLOMON AND THE LADIES OF THE HAREM INTRODUCED[3]
(3: 6–11)

3: 6   *What[4] is that coming up from the wilderness[5]*
    like a column[6] of smoke,
  perfumed with myrrh and frankincense,
    with all fragrant powders of the merchant?
  7 *Ah, it is the litter of[7] Solomon!*
    Sixty valiant men surround it
    of the valiant men of Israel,
  8 *all of them armed with swords,*
    expert in war,
  each with his sword at his hip
    against the alarm by night.

NOTE.—The chapter and verse divisions indicated in the present translation are those of the traditional text of the Song. The significant change in the order of the lines is the transposition of 3: 6—4: 6 to follow 1: 1 (see above, pp. 9 ff.). The textual and critical notes appear on pp. 59–88.

3: 9   *(King Solomon made himself a palanquin[8]*
      from the wood of Lebanon.

10   *He made its supports[9] of silver,*
      its back of gold,
      its seat of purple,
      its interior inlaid with ebony.[10])

11   *Go forth, O Daughters of Jerusalem,[11]*
      and gaze upon King Solomon,
  upon the crown with which his mother[12] crowned him
      on the day of his wedding ceremony,[13]
      on the day of the gladness of his heart.[14]

SOLOMON TO THE SERVANT GIRL FROM SHUNEM[15]
(4: 1–6)

4: 1   *Behold, you are beautiful, shepherd girl,[16]*
      you are very[17] beautiful!
      Your eyes are doves (behind your veil).[18]
  Your hair is like a flock of goats
      reclining on[19] the slopes of Gilead.

2   *Your teeth are like a flock of ewes herded together[20]*
      that have come up from the washing,
  every one of which has twins;
      not one is bereaved among them.

3   *Your lips are like a scarlet thread,*
      and your mouth[21] is comely.[22]
  Your temples[23] are like a sliced[24] pomegranate
                (behind your veil).[25]

4   *Your neck is like a tower of David[26]*
      built for an arsenal,[27]
  whereon hang a thousand bucklers,
      every one a warrior's shield.

4: 5 *Your breasts are like two fawns,*
twins of a gazelle,
that feed among the lilies.

6 *Until the day breathe[28] cool*
and the shadows stretch away
I will hie me to the mountain of myrrh[29]
and the hill of frankincense.

(Solomon offers the girl a kiss,
from which she recoils.)

COURT LADIES (QUEENS AND CONCUBINES)[30]
(1 : 2–4)

1: 2 *O that he would kiss me with the kisses of his mouth,*
for your caresses are better[31] than wine.

3 *Your anointing oils[32] are delicate for perfume,*
your presence is like perfumed oil poured out;
of course the servant girls[33] must love you.

4 *Draw me after you, let us make haste;*
the King brought me[34] into his chambers.
We exult and rejoice in you,
we extol your caresses more than wine;
rightly they cannot but love you.

THE SERVANT GIRL TO THE COURT LADIES[35]
(1 : 5–7)

5 *Very dark am I, though comely,*
O Daughters of Jerusalem,
as tents of Kedar,[36]
as curtains of Solomon.[37]

43

1: 6   *Do not regard me, because I am swarthy,*
      because the sun has blazed upon[38] me.
  My mother's sons were angry with me,
      they made me keeper of the vineyards.
  Alas,[39] my own vineyard have I not kept!

7   *Tell me, you whom my soul loves,*
      where you pasture your flock,
      where you make it to rest at noon;
  for why should I be as one that is veiled[40]
      beside the flocks of your companions?

COURT LADIES TO THE GIRL[41]

(1:8)

8   *If you know not,*
      O fairest among women,[42]
  go forth at the heels[43] of the flock
  and pasture your kids
  beside the shepherds' tents.

SOLOMON TO THE GIRL

(1: 9–11)

9   *To my mare[44] in my chariot[45] of Pharaoh*
      have I likened you, shepherd girl.[16]

10   *Your cheeks,[46] how[47] comely with ornaments,*
      your neck with strings of jewels!

11   *We will make you ornaments of gold*
      studded with silver.

THE GIRL TO THE COURT LADIES[48]
(1:12–14)

1:12 *While the King was in the royal procession*[49]
    my nard gave forth its fragrance.

13 *Dodai*[50] *is to me as a bag of myrrh*
    that lies between my breasts.

14 *Dodai is to me as a cluster of henna blossoms*
    from the vineyards of Engedi.[51]

SOLOMON TO THE GIRL[52]
(1:15)

15 *Behold, you are beautiful, shepherd girl,*
    you are very beautiful!
    Your eyes are doves.

THE GIRL (IN AN APOSTROPHE)[53]
(1:16—2:1)

16 *Behold, you are beautiful, Dodai,*
    truly lovely.
    Yea, our couch is nature's own greenness.[54]

17 *The beams of our house are cedars,*
    our rafters[55] *are fir trees.*

2:1 *I am only a rose*[56] *of Sharon,*
    a lily of the valleys.

SOLOMON TO THE GIRL[57]
(2:2)

2 *As a lily among brambles,*
    so is my shepherd girl among the Daughters.[58]

45

THE GIRL TO THE COURT LADIES[59]
(2 : 3—3 : 5; 4 : 7—5 : 8)

2 : 3   *As an apple tree among the trees of the wood,*
    so is Dodai among the sons.[60]
  With great delight I sat in his shadow,
    and his fruit was sweet to my taste.

4   *He brought me to the banqueting house,*
    and the look in his eyes[61] *was love.*

5   *Stay me with raisin cakes,*
    refresh me with apples,
    for I am sick with love.

6   *O that his left hand were under my head*
    and his right hand did embrace me!

7   *I adjure you,*[62] *O Daughters of Jerusalem,*
    by the gazelles or by the hinds of the field,
  that you stir not up nor awaken love
    until it please.

8   *The voice of Dodai!*[63]
    See, there he comes,
  bounding over the mountains,
    skipping over the hills.

9   *Dodai is like a gazelle*
    or a young stag.
  Ah, there he stands
    behind our wall,
  gazing in at the windows,
    peering through the lattice.

10   *Dodai sings*[64] *and is calling*[65] *to me,*

46

"Arise, my beautiful shepherdess,
and come away,
2:11 *for, see, the winter is past,*
the rain is over and gone.
12 *The flowers appear on the earth,*
the time of singing has come,
and the note of the turtle dove
is heard in our land.
13 *The fig tree puts forth its figs,*
and the vines are in bloom;
they diffuse perfume.
Arise, my beautiful shepherdess,
and come away.
14 *"O my dove in the clefts of the crag,*
in the hidden coverts of the cliff,
let me see your form,
make me to hear your voice,
for sweet is your voice,
and your form is comely.
15 *"Catch us foxes,*
little foxes,
that are destroying the vineyards,
for our vineyards are in full bloom."
16 *Dodai is mine and I am his;*
he pastures his flock among the lilies.
17 *Until the day breathe cool*
and the shadows stretch away[28]
roam,[66] *O Dodai, like a gazelle*
or a young stag upon rugged[67] *mountains.*

(Reminiscence of first dream)[68]

(3: 1–4)

3: 1 *Upon my bed by night*
I sought him whom my soul loves;
I sought him, but I found him not;
I called him, but he gave no answer.[69]

2 *"I will arise now and go about the city,*
in the markets and in the concourses,
to seek him whom my soul loves."
I sought him, but I found him not.

3 *The watchmen found me,*
who go about in the city.
"Have you seen him whom my soul loves?"

4 *Scarcely had I passed them*
when I found him whom my soul loves.
I held him and would not let him go
until I had brought him to my mother's house
and to the abode of her that conceived me.

5 *I adjure you, O Daughters of Jerusalem,*
by the gazelles or by the hinds of the field,
that you stir not up nor awaken love
until it please.

(Reminiscence of a second dream)[70]

(4: 7—5: 2a)

4: 7 [*The voice of Dodai!*][71]

(The lover to the girl)

You are altogether beautiful, O shepherdess,
and there is no spot in you.

48

4: 8   Come[72] from Lebanon,[73] make an end,
     come, from Lebanon come.
Flee from the top of Amana,
     from the top of Senir-Hermon,[74]
from dens of lions,
     from mountains of leopards.

9   You have ravished my heart, my sister, bride,[75]
     you have ravished my heart
with one glance of your eyes,
     with one jewel of your necklace.

10   How sweet are your caresses,
     my sister, bride,
how much better are your caresses than wine,
     and the fragrance of your oils than all perfume.

11   Your lips distil nectar, O bride.
     Honey and milk are under your tongue,
and the scent of your garments
     is like the scent of Lebanon.

12   A garden locked is my sister, bride,
     a garden locked, a fountain sealed,

13   whose parting gifts[76] are rows[77] of pomegranate trees,
     with all precious fruits,
     henna with nard,

14   nard and saffron, calamus and cinnamon,
     with all trees of frankincense,
myrrh and aloes,
     with all chief spices,

15   a garden fountain, a well of living water,
     and flowing streams from Lebanon.

(The girl's dream response)[78]

4: 16 *Awake, O North Wind,*
      and come, O South Wind!
  Blow upon my garden
      that its spices may distil.
  Let Dodai come to his garden
      and eat its choice fruits.

(The lover's dream reply)[79]

5: 1 *I come[80] to my garden, my sister, bride,*
      I gather my myrrh with my spice,
  I eat my honeycomb with my honey,
      I drink my wine with my milk.
  The friends eat and drink,
      and the kinsmen[81] are surfeited with wine.

(The girl's explanation to the Court)

2 *I had been asleep, but my heart was awake.[82]*

(Reminiscence of a third dream)[83]
(5: 2b–7)

  The voice of Dodai! he is knocking.
  "Open to me, my sister, my shepherdess,
      my dove, my perfect one,
  for my head is wet with dew,
      my locks with the drops of the night."

3 *I had put off my garment,*
      how should I put it on?
  I had bathed my feet,
      how should I soil them?[84]

5: 4   *Dodai put his hand to the latch,*[85]
      and my heart went out to him.

  5   *I arose to open to Dodai,*
      and my hands dropped myrrh,
    and my fingers choice myrrh
      upon the wards of the lock.

  6   *I opened to Dodai,*
      but Dodai had turned and gone.
      My soul failed me when he was not there.[86]
    I sought him, but I found him not;
      I called him, but he gave no answer.

  7   *The watchmen who go about in the city found me;*
      they beat me, they wounded me,
    they took away my mantle,
      those watchmen of the walls!

  8   *I adjure you, O Daughters of Jerusalem,*[87]
      if you should find Dodai,
    what would you tell him?—
      that I am sick with love.

THE LADIES TO THE GIRL[88]
(5:9)

  9   *What is your Dodai compared with David,*[89]
      O fairest among women?
    What is your Dodai compared with David,
      that you do thus adjure us?

THE GIRL TO THE LADIES[90]
(5: 10–16)

 10   *Dodai is all radiant and ruddy,*
      distinguished among ten thousand.

5: 11 *His head is the most fine gold.*
   His locks are wavy,
   black as a raven.

12 *His eyes are like doves*
   beside springs of water,
   bathed in milk,
   full of luster.[91]

13 *His cheeks are like banks of spices*
   wafting[92] *perfume.*
   His lips are lilies
   yielding choice myrrh.

14 *His arms*[93] *are rounded gold*
   set with jewels.
   His body is ivory work[94]
   encrusted with sapphires.[95]

15 *His legs are marble columns*
   set upon golden bases.
   His aspect is like Lebanon,
   choice as the cedars.

16 *His speech is most sweet,*
   yea, he is altogether lovely.
   This is Dodai, and this is my friend,
   O Daughters of Jerusalem.

THE LADIES TO THE GIRL[96]
(6: 1)

6: 1 *Whither has your Dodai gone,*
   O fairest among women?
   Whither has your Dodai turned aside,
   that we may seek him with you?

THE GIRL TO THE LADIES[97]
(6:2–3)

6: 2 *Dodai has gone down to his garden,*
to the beds of spices,
to pasture his flock in the gardens
and to gather lilies.

3 *I belong to Dodai and Dodai is mine;*
he pastures his flock among the lilies.

SOLOMON TO THE GIRL[98]
(6:4–10)

4 *You are beautiful, shepherd girl, as Tirzah,[99]*
comely as Jerusalem,
awe-inspiring as an embattled host.[100]

5 *Turn away your eyes from me,*
for they discomfit me.
Your hair is like a flock of goats
reclining on the slopes of Gilead.

6 *Your teeth are like a flock of ewes*
that go up from the washing,
whereof every one has twins;
not one is bereaved among them.

7 *Your temples are like a sliced pomegranate.[101]*

8 *There are sixty queens and eighty concubines*
and servant girls without number.[102]

9 *One[103] is my dove, my perfection,*
the only one of her mother,
flawless to her that bore her.
The Daughters saw her and praised her,
the queens and concubines,[104] and they extolled
her:

53

6: 10   *"Who is this like the blush of dawn,*[105]
       fair as the moon, bright as the sun,
       awe-inspiring as an embattled host?"[100]

THE GIRL'S EXPLANATION[106]
(6: 11–12)

11 *To the nut orchard I had gone down*
      to look at the fresh growth[107] *of the valley,*
   to see whether the vines had budded,
      whether the pomegranates were in bloom.
12 *Or ever I was aware my fancy*[108] *had brought*[109] *me*
     to the chariots of my princely[110] *people.*

MEMBERS OF THE HAREM[111]
(6: 13ab)

13 *Stay, stay,*[112] *O Shunammite,*[113]
    stay, stay, that we may look upon you.

THE GIRL'S PROTEST[114]
(6: 13cd)

Why should you look upon a Shunammite
   as upon a dance of two companies?[115]

THE LADIES TO THE GIRL[116]
(7: 1–5)

7: 1 *How graceful your feet in sandals,*[117]
     O princely daughter!
    Your rounded thighs are like jewels,
     the work of a master hand.

7: 2 *Your body[118] is a well-rounded bowl,*
may it never lack mixed wine.
Your waist[119] is like a heap of wheat
set about with lilies.

3 *Your breasts are like two fawns,*
twins of a gazelle.

4 *Your neck is like an ivory tower.*
Your eyes are pools in Heshbon,
by the gate of Bath-rabbim.
Your nose is like a tower of Lebanon
overlooking Damascus.

5 *Your head crowns[120] you like Carmel,*
and your flowing locks are like purple.
A king is held captive in the tresses.[121]

SOLOMON TO THE GIRL[122]
(7: 6–9a)

6 *How fair and pleasant you are,*
O love, among delightsome things!

7 *You are stately as[123] a palm tree,*
and your breasts like its clusters.

8 *I say I will ascend the palm tree,*
I will lay hold of its branches.
May your breasts be as clusters of the vine,
and the scent of your breath[124] like apples,

9 *and your kisses[125] like the best wine—*

THE GIRL'S FINAL REPLY TO KING AND COURT[126]
(7: 9b—8: 4)

—flowing[127] for Dodai, as is his right,[128]
gliding over[129] lips and teeth.[130]

7: 10   *I belong to Dodai,*
      and to me is his desire.

  11   **Come, Dodai,**
      O that we might[131] go forth into the fields
      and lodge in the villages,

  12   *that we might go out early to the vineyards*
      and see whether the vines have budded,
  whether the grape blossoms have opened
      and the pomegranates are in bloom.
  There would I give you a token[132] of my love.

  13   *The mandrakes diffuse fragrance,*
      and over our doors are all the choice fruits,
  new as well as old,
      O Dodai, which I have laid up for you.

8: 1   *O that you were[133] like a brother to me,*
      that nursed at my mother's breast!
  If I found you in the street[134] I would kiss you,
      and none would despise me.

  2   *I would lead you, bring you*
      to the house of my mother, who was ever my
         instructor.[135]
  I would give you to drink of spiced wine,
      of the new wine of my pomegranates.

  3   *O that his left hand were under my head*
      and that his right hand did embrace me!

  4   *I adjure you, O Daughters of Jerusalem,*
      why will you stir up and why awaken love
      until it please?[136]

PART II

RURAL VILLAGE SCENE AT SHUNEM[2]
(8:5–14)

THE GIRL'S BROTHERS[137]
(8:5ab)

8: 5 *Who is that[138] coming up from the wilderness,[139]*
arm in arm[140] with Dodo?[141]

THE LOVER TO THE GIRL[142]
(8:5c–e)

Under this apple tree I awakened you.
Yonder is your mother's home,
where you were born.[143]

THE GIRL TO THE LOVER[144]
(8:6–12)

6 *Set me as a seal upon your heart,*
as a seal upon your arm,
for strong as death is love,
ardent love[145] as mighty as Sheol;
its flashes are bolts of flame,
of consuming fire.[146]
7 *Many waters cannot quench love,*
neither can torrents sweep it away.
If a man would give all the wealth
of his house for love,
men would utterly despise him.[147]
8 *"We have a little sister,*

57

and she has no breasts.
What shall we do for our sister
on the day when she will be spoken for?

8: 9 If she be a wall,
we shall build upon it a battlement of silver,
but if she be a door,
we shall inclose it with planks of cedar." [148]

10 I was indeed a wall,
and my breasts like its towers; [149]
then was I in his eyes,
as one that finds peace.

11 Solomon has [150] a vineyard at Baal-hamon;
he let out the vineyard to keepers;
each one for its fruit
was to bring a thousand pieces of silver.

12 My vineyard, my very own, is for myself; [151]
the thousand for you, O Solomon,
and two hundred for the caretakers of the fruit.

THE LOVER TO THE GIRL [152]
(8:13)

13 O you that sit in the garden, [153]
the companions wait for your voice;
let me hear it.

THE GIRL TO THE LOVER [154]
(8:14)

14 Flee away, O Dodai,
and be like a gazelle
or a young stag
upon the fragrant [155] mountains.

TEXTUAL AND CRITICAL NOTES

[1] As a title "The Song of Songs" is clearly intended to be a (1:1)
superlative, like "the holy of holies" and "the king of kings."
The poem is thus declared to be the best of all songs. This
heading, however, is hardly to be regarded as original (cf.
W. W. Cannon, *The Song of Songs* [Cambridge University Press,
1913], p. 4), but is, rather, to be considered the result of a
later evaluation of the poem. Moreover, there are good
grounds for believing that the superlative is bound up with the
late gloss (1:1), traditionally rendered "which is Solomon's."
Originally this expression was probably not intended to indicate
authorship (cf. Introduction, pp. 5–6), but once it came to be
so interpreted, the work was not just a song of Solomon but by
all odds the most distinguished of all songs that have been attributed to him. When his name is removed from the title, however, the superlative character of the poem is by no means
unequivocal. It is first of all a purely secular poem, in which
the heroine and her shepherd lover have, in themselves, no
national significance, and in which Solomon plays a relatively
minor part. To justify its claim to uniqueness by its style or
diction, its delight in nature, or its portrayal of romantic love,
or by all of these combined, is to rely upon very doubtful criteria,
especially for ancient times. But if we lay aside the superlative
force in the phrase, what we have left is a "song of songs," that
is, a song made up of part songs, sung by different characters or
groups of characters. This at least proves to be an accurate
description of the piece and may well have been the original
intent, for in literary form the Song approximates the modern
oratorio in certain respects, while to the extent that it takes on
a formal setting and calls for dramatic action, as, for example,
in 3:11; 4:6; 7:6–9a, it partakes of the qualities of opera.
Hebrew had no name or category for either art.

59

(1:2—8:4)   [2] On the articulation of this scene see Introduction, pp. 7–13.

(3:6—4:6)   [3] This section accomplishes the introduction of Solomon and the ladies of the harem (3:6–11). The passage 3:6—4:6 in the traditional arrangement of the Song fails entirely to serve as an introduction; it merely interrupts the context. Yet the section 1:2 ff. imperatively needs an introduction, for women and a king are present, but who and where they are and why they say what they do cannot be discerned in the traditional context.

The advantage of an introduction at the opening of a work is self-evident, and the justification for transferring 3:6—4:6 to the beginning is the light which the new arrangement throws upon the section 1:2 ff., as well as upon the poem as a whole. For further discussion of the problem and an explanation of the displacement in the traditional text see Introduction, pp. 13–16.

(3:6)   [4] "What": The interrogative pronoun *mî* is generally used of persons, but sometimes, as here, of persons and things (cf. Gen. 33:8; Mic. 1:5).

[5] "coming up from the wilderness": The route followed was probably the road running southeast from Jerusalem across the Kidron Valley (cf. 2 Sam. 15:23). The phrase does not necessarily indicate that the King had been away on a journey; it may be only a reference to a royal procession (of which 1 Kings 1:38–40 describes an earlier phase) in and about the city in connection with Solomon's coronation ceremonies (cf. 3:11).

[6] "column": The Hebrew has the plural. This might be the plural used for the singular, as frequently in the Song, but twenty manuscripts and LXX read the singular.

(3:7)   [7] The consistent use of the relative particle *š* for *'ašer* throughout the Song has been taken as an argument for the poem's late date, but the argument proves too much; for if the Song were as late as this usage is made to imply that it is, it should exhibit many other signs of lateness, which, however, are not found. The inference, moreover, is unnecessary, since the particle *š*, corresponding to Akkadian *š a*, is also a mark of early North Palestinian Hebrew (cf. Gen. 6: 3; Jd. 5: 7; 6: 17; 7: 12; 8: 26; 2 Kings 6: 11; see F. R. Blake, "The Form of Verbs after Waw in Hebrew," *Journal of Biblical Literature,* 65 [1946]: 57, who regards *š* as the popular form, appearing occasionally in the earlier books, and *'ašer* as the one regularly used for literary purposes, and cf. H. Bauer and P. Leander, *Historische Grammatik der hebraische Sprache* [Halle a. S., 1918], p. 462).

[8] "palanquin": *a p p i r y o n* is a Semitic adaptation or corrup- (3: 9–10) tion of Greek *ph o r i o n*. This word has been used as a basis for dating the Song in the Hellenistic period. But vss. 9–10 are probably a gloss (cf. Cannon, *op. cit.,* p. 135) from the Greek period. There are a number of circumstances that support this view: (1) Solomon's conveyance is described in v. 7 as a "litter" (strictly, "couch"), whereas the palanquin of vss. 9–10 is much more elaborate and ornate. (2) Vss. 9–10 interrupt the context by diverting attention from the approaching procession, and v. 11 connects directly with v. 8. (3) This is the one place in the Song where there is evident delight in describing the splendor and magnificence associated with the name of Solomon. And, (4), the author, quite contrary to his practice, revels in minutiae until the text is fairly top-heavy. The passage is comparable to the very certain gloss in Is. 3: 18–23. Our two verses may well have been a marginal note jotted down by someone who felt that Solomon must have had a better conveyance than the simple litter of v. 7, and that this fact should be recorded.

[9] "supports": A more literal meaning is "columns"; they may (3: 10) have been either posts, like the legs of a bed, designed to keep the litter proper off the ground, or supports for a canopy above.

¹⁰ *'ahabah*, "love," is, as many scholars maintain, to be read *hobni*, "ebony." Owing to the change to *'ahabah*, the Hebrew felt it necessary to insert "from" before "Daughters"; the phrase that follows then had to be a part of v. 10, whereas, in accord with LXX, it should begin v. 11. In this reading the Northern girl always, appropriately, addresses the ladies of the royal harem.

(3:11)   ¹¹ The Hebrew has inserted "daughters of Zion" here because of the transfer of "Daughters of Jerusalem" to v. 10. For the meaning of the latter phrase see Introduction, pp. 7–8.

¹² "his mother": The activities of Bathsheba described in I Kings 1:15–39 deal with the essentials of the event referred to here.

¹³ "wedding ceremony": For the meaning here see Introduction, p. 7.

¹⁴ This line is connected with the preceding by waw *explicativum* (omitted in translation; cf. A. O. Ehrlich, *Randglossen zur hebraischen Bibel* [Leipzig, 1914], VII, 9), since the three lines *c–e* all refer to the same episode; they thus fix the time setting of the Song as being related to Solomon's coronation ceremonies.

(4:1–6)   ¹⁵ "servant girl from Shunem": See notes 33 and 113. In 4:1–6 the harem scene, one of great regal splendor, takes on striking dramatic interest. The 140 queens and concubines in their best finery have been summoned, together with countless servant girls (cf. 6:8), to greet their lord. Solomon enters their presence in full coronation regalia. This is to be his wedding ceremony. No bride is mentioned, and none need be under the circumstances, for he has presumably come to make formal acknowledgment of the entire harem and formal recognition of its relation to him. Some gesture or greeting to the harem or to its leading members would, however, surely be expected, but Solomon completely ignores the harem as a whole and, instead, directs his entire attention and his words to one of the prettiest of the servant girls; from that point everything in the poem focuses upon this young peasant girl.

[16] "shepherd girl": On this rendering and the reasons for it (4:1) see Introduction, pp. 18 f.

[17] The repetition of the compliment gives it added emphasis, which is expressed in English by "very."

[18] "(behind your veil)": This is probably a gloss, for the following reasons: (1) The phrase does not occur with the same metaphor in 1:15. (2) The girl speaks of being veiled in 1:7 as a mark of dishonor. (3) There appear to be metrical grounds for the deletion of the words, as recommended by R. Kittel in *Biblia Hebraica* (2d ed.; Leipzig, 1913). (4) Since this passage is all a part of the harem scene, there is no occasion for any use whatever of the veil. (5) LXX seems to realize the situation and cuts the Gordian knot by reading "without your veil" or, more freely, "now that your veil is removed." And, (6), there is no reason why any of the servant girls of the palace should ever be supposed to wear veils, and, above all, why they should be veiled from Solomon.

[19] "reclining on": The meaning of the Hebrew verb is uncertain. The word is found only here. The nearest cognate suggests "sit" or "recline on" (literally "from"), perhaps with reference to the steep slopes, which might give the sense "clinging to." The comparison of the girl's hair to a flock of goats would have been straightforward and legitimate if mention of the slopes of Gilead had been omitted. As the image stands, the mountain background is, in reference to a girl's head, too large for the goats, for if they are bunched together there are too many slopes bare of goats, but if they are scattered the emphasis in the figure falls upon the girl's hairs rather than her hair. Thus the figure is bizarre, if not grotesque, possibly by intent of the author (cf. Introduction, pp. 37–38).

(4:2) [20] "herded together": The traditional rendering of *qeṣu-both* as "newly shorn" or "ready to be shorn" is unwarranted. The Hebrew term occurs again only in 2 Kings 6:6, where it signifies "to cut off a stick." The word used for shearing is an entirely different word. But if we reverse two consonants, we get *qebuṣoth*, which gives the appropriate meaning suggested here, for when sheep go up from the washing, they tend to scatter and have to be gathered together. The figure is still far from happy, since it fails to convey a picture of the orderliness of a good set of teeth, and suggests, rather, that they are jumbled together. In short, the simile is inaccurate and clumsy, and the King pays the girl a very doubtful compliment when he thus goes out of his way to emphasize the fact that she has a full set of teeth. Had he said her teeth were as white as wool, the figure would have been adequate.

(4:3) [21] "mouth": *midbar*, to denote the organ of speech, is found only here.

[22] "comely": The word occurs also in 1:5. It would have been more natural and appropriate if the speaker had said *yapha*, meaning "beautiful" or "lovely," but he did not go so far with his compliment.

[23] "temples": Etymologically the Hebrew word means "thinness," which is particularly applicable to the temples. It occurs outside the Song only in Jd. 4:21, 22, and 5:26, where it can mean only "temple." The attempt by P. Jöuon, in his *Le Cantique des cantiques* (Rome, 1919), *ad loc.*, to make this word refer here to the upper part of the cheek has no linguistic basis, but rests solely on the ground that it would not have been appropriate to compare the girl's temples with the bright colors of a section of pomegranate and that Solomon, therefore, must have been referring to her cheeks. This is gratuitous. If Solomon had meant to refer to her cheeks, he would undoubtedly have used *leḥi* (cf. Lam. 1:2). Many of the

King's figures are too weak to base any argument a priori on their appropriateness. As a matter of fact, the comparison is at best virtually inapplicable, since the girl's exposed skin, according to her own statement (cf. 1: 5), was burned practically black.

[24] "sliced": Literally, the Hebrew wording denotes a slice or a cross section of a pomegranate. The assumption that because the same word is used for "millstone" the term here indicates the two halves of a pomegranate (cf. Jöuon, *op. cit.*) rests upon a false concept of mills in early Israel; actually the upper millstone was small enough to be grasped in the hands for rubbing on a much larger "saddle quern" below (cf. G. A. Barton, *Archaeology and the Bible* [6th ed.; Philadelphia, 1933], p. 181). Moreover, the halves of a pomegranate would not aptly describe the temples, as Jöuon is well aware.

[25] For the reason for this parenthesis, "(behind your veil)," see note 18.

[26] "a tower of David": We know of no particular historical (4:4) "tower of David," but the account of David's placing garrisons in Syria and Edom (cf. 2 Sam. 8: 6, 14) would indicate that he fortified a number of places besides Jerusalem; hence the rendering here.

[27] The word *t a l p i y y o th* is found only here, and the meaning is uncertain. The context calls for a structure used for storing weapons of war, whether captured trophies or new equipment; hence the rendering "arsenal." The figure, applied to the girl's neck, makes her a Brobdingnagian, and is so outlandish and extreme that it reflects on Solomon rather than on the maiden. It could hardly have failed to call forth at least a subdued titter from the assembled harem.

[28] "breathe": The reference is to a breeze characteristic of (4:6) Palestine. It might be either the breeze that begins about the middle of the forenoon or the one that blows at early evening.

Mention of shadows in the next line has a bearing on which breeze is meant, for shadows are not noticeable in midmorning but become so, especially in a hilly country like Palestine, in the late afternoon. At that time they stretch out swiftly across the landscape. Their speed is such that they are poetically described as fleeing, which does not mean that they either disappear or cease to be. LXX interprets this as "stretching out," and does not, therefore, require a different reading from the present Hebrew. For a similar description in English literature see line 3 of the verses introducing Canto IV in Tennyson's *Princess*: "The long light shakes across the lakes." Since the reference thus appears to be to the early evening breeze, "breathe cool" gives the sense (cf. Gen. 3:8), and the meaning of the two lines is "until evening."

[29] "mountain of myrrh, etc.": The language here is highly figurative. What was intended can best be determined by the sequel in 1:2 ff., which definitely implies that the king offered the girl a kiss; that incident would plausibly make the mountain of myrrh and the hill of frankincense refer to the girl's cheeks; cf. 5:13*ab*, which is the same type of figure, but lacks the extreme exaggeration. These figures in 4:6 are, however, in good accord with 4:4. See Introduction, p. 37.

(1:2 ff.)   [30] See Introduction, p. 10, in regard to the sequence of the lines that follow and the speakers. The frequent change of person and number in these verses indicates that the court ladies are talking among themselves in the presence of the King. He had not addressed or openly noticed them. Nevertheless, their words, whether they refer to him in the second or the third person, are meant for Solomon to hear, but he makes no reply either to individuals or to the group.

(1:2)   [31] "better": The rendering "sweeter" would go well with "caresses," but sweet wine in Hebrew is technically not wine at all.

³² "anointing oils": Literally, "oils." These are such oils (1:3) as were used on the person in any way; they are said to have been perfumed. In line *b* "your presence [literally, 'name'] is like oil," refers to the King's own oils; hence the rendering "perfumed oil."

³³ "servant girls": The word *'alamoth* means young women of marriageable age, whether married or unmarried. Any wife could be so designated, at least until she had borne a child. In the Song the word has a special meaning, which is defined in 6: 8, where Solomon describes his harem as composed of sixty queens, eighty concubines, and *'alamoth* without number. Such a large group of wives of the first and second rank would naturally require a large staff of servants, all of whom would have to be able-bodied women (no men servants being allowed in the harem). The legal status of these servants was explicit in Israel (cf. Ex. 21: 7–11): they necessarily became subordinate wives; in Solomon's harem they would be wives of the third class (cf. Gen. 30: 3, 9; Ps. 45: 14). The social status of such women was otherwise nondescript, and if they had not borne children they could be discharged at will and without redress (cf. Ex. 21: 11). The term "maiden" in English implies virginity and is therefore inappropriate here, whereas the phrase "servant girls" expresses their main function in the harem.

Thus the court ladies (queens and concubines) are speaking here not of maidens or young women in general, but of their own domestic servants in the palace household, and they are saying, literally, "therefore the servant girls love you." Yet this is not a sudden flat assertion, but is based on the attractiveness they have just attributed to the King; hence the rendering "must love." Furthermore, "therefore," though a literal translation, is too formal and dignified in English. The colloquial speech and the intuitive logic of the harem are more

67

nearly expressed by "of course." But why this emphasis?
Normally it was to the interest of the superior wives to keep
the husband's relation to their female subordinates as much out
of sight and out of mind as possible. Here the ladies go out
of their way to affirm that the servant girls must love him, and
(v. 4e) that rightly they cannot do otherwise. As we have
seen, Solomon has just addressed the girl, and in the restored
context the indications are that he concluded his first speech to
her by offering her an embrace and a kiss (cf. 1:2a). If she
had responded unreservedly to the King's gesture, the ladies
would have had no grounds to question the loyalty and devotion
of the servant girls to their lord; and in that event it is highly
improbable that they would have spoken as they did, since to
have done so would have been to give open encouragement to
all the maidservants to follow the Shunammite girl's example.
But if the latter recoiled and shrank back from the King's advances, the words spoken by the women in this passage would
be entirely understandable, since such sentiments would serve
to improve their own standing with the King, first, by rebuking
the girl for a lack of loving respect and good taste in his presence
(of which they were no doubt secretly glad), and, secondly, by
showing that their own glowing estimate of the King's favors
and their fervid attachment to him went far beyond any such
mere dutiful love. Because of her action they can now safely
affirm that all the servants ought to have the devotion the
Shunammite lacks. And there is a further delicate hint in the
imperfects used in v. 4 that they themselves are always ready to
manifest their devotion whenever they are given opportunity.

(1:4)   [34] "brought me": Line b is uttered as a justification for a,
and says in effect: "I am one whom the King brought into his
chambers." The words are, accordingly, those of a favorite
wife. The sequence of thought in the present arrangement
knits together 3:6 and 1:2 ff. and makes it almost compulsory

68

that the speakers in 1: 2–4 be the court ladies. The correctness of this sequence, including its implications in regard to the attitude of the girl toward the King, is further confirmed by her first speech (1: 5–7; cf. note 59).

[35] This speech is addressed, not to the King, but to the court (1: 5–7) ladies, who are invoked as "Daughters of Jerusalem." Nevertheless, the reasons for the girl's words are to be found in the King's speech. They are, therefore, though addressed to the entire court, an answer to his remarks, since he, also, was present; and they are put thus adroitly so that they cannot be taken as an affront to the King himself. This is clear from the fact that though Solomon has emphasized her beauty she points out to the ladies that she is as black as a goat's-hair tent, that is, she is a peasant, and she offers this as an argument why the court should not regard her. Yet the women had not previously noticed her. It was Solomon who had singled her out, and he had given her his undivided attention. The girl then explains any coolness shown to the King by a soulful apostrophe to an absent shepherd lover for whom she expresses heartfelt love and longing, and she closes with the strong hint that her present position at the palace is compromising her character.

[36] "tents of Kedar": This is a reference to the black goat's- (1: 5) hair tents of the Bedouin; Kedar was a well-known nomad tribe of northern Arabia.

[37] "curtains of Solomon": It is notable that the Song puts the rich hangings of Solomon on a level with the rough goat's-hair coverings of the Bedouin tents. This is characteristic of the poet's disregard of and contempt for the outward splendor and magnificence of Solomon.

[38] "blazed upon": Literally, "scorched." The present read- (1: 6) ing is supported by Aquila's *sunekausen* and Theodotion's *periephrukse,* which go back to the Aramaic *šadaf* rather than to the Hebrew *šazaf.*

³⁹ "Alas": This word is supplied because the line expresses the girl's deep emotional reaction to her situation, a reaction which reveals its full force only with 8: 12.

(1:7)   ⁴⁰ "veiled": The figure is clear in Gen. 38: 14, where the veiled woman is one of ill repute. The girl is saying that, because of her devotion to her lover, even her presence in the harem compromises her. The rather common practice of correcting the text to read "stray" or "wander" has no justification, since it gives no such clear or appropriate picture supported by literary usage.

(1: 8 ff.)   ⁴¹ From this point the court ladies have their attention fixed upon the girl and to all intents and purposes lose sight of the King, although he continues to address the maiden from time to time. Each time he does so she directs her reply at the ladies. Their preoccupation with her is part of the art of the poem, to keep the heroine in the limelight throughout. In this instance (1: 8) they doubtless seize upon her reference to her shepherd lover as the quickest way of disposing of her objections, and they ironically suggest: "Why, then, do you not go and become a shepherdess?"

(1: 8)   ⁴² "fairest among women": This is a very remarkable phrase in itself, and it becomes progressively more remarkable when one considers that it was uttered by women, agreed upon by a relatively large group of them, applied by the top-ranking ladies of the realm to one of their own maidservants, and addressed to a servant whom the lord and husband of them all was at that very time showering with compliments and endearments in their presence. It is still more striking, under the circumstances, that these women should go beyond their lord in praising her beauty, and it is most extraordinary of all that they should never think of addressing her by any other epithet, even though at the outset she had protested to them that she was as black as a Bedouin's tent.

70

The explanation of their surprising behavior must be sought in the poet's intention. What justified the representation of such an extreme attitude and what was the author's purpose? The answer lies in the existence of a well-known tradition in early Israel to the effect that, during the final days of King David, a beautiful maiden was sought throughout the land to care for him in his last illness. The girl selected, said to be exquisitely lovely, was a peasant girl from Shunem in North Israel. She was brought to Jerusalem and ministered in the palace as a servant to King David (1 Kings 1: 3–4). Furthermore, it is said that Solomon at one time thought highly of her and probably considered taking her into his harem (cf. 1 Kings 2: 22), although there is no record that he ever did so.

The poet has added only two things. First, he has made the girl's beauty an absolute superlative and, secondly, he has made the queens and the concubines of Solomon's huge harem the sponsors of that superlative. The effect in glorifying the girl is as apparent as the author's corresponding disparagement of the royal establishment of Solomon.

[43] "go forth at the heels": This is only another way of saying "become a shepherdess." The equally possible rendering "follow in the tracks" would point, rather, to the girl's finding the shepherd, whereas the sequel makes no mention of him, but dwells only upon the duties of a shepherdess.

[44] "my mare": The Hebrew form is explicit as pointed, and (1:9) the versions agree with it. There is no reason to doubt the meaning, since the comparison of a woman to a favorite mare is classic in the Near East. The only unusual thing about the figure here is that the mare is harnessed, and hitched to the royal chariot. This feature is the contribution of the poet and must be taken into account in his portraiture of Solomon. By changing the consonantal text it is possible to read "to a mare of Pharaoh's chariots," but a somewhat serious difficulty

71

is that the word used for chariot properly signifies, as Ehrlich points out (*op. cit.*, p. 4), a war chariot, and the war chariots of the Egyptians were famous for being drawn by stallions.

[45] "my chariot": This rendering does not require a change in the consonantal text, but, as read, the word is an abbreviation for *rikbi rekeb Par'oh*, "my chariot, namely, a chariot of Pharaoh" (cf. Gesenius–Kautzsch, *Hebrew Grammar* [Oxford, 1910], 128d and Lev. 26:42), which has the force of such present-day expressions as "Lincoln car."

(1:10)   [46] "Your cheeks": Commentators have been puzzled to explain the cheek ornaments. The suggestion of Jöuon (*op. cit.*) that this verse and the following one continue the figure of the mare with decorated bridle and trappings does much to relieve the difficulty and to make the two verses seem straightforward.

[47] "how": This rendering follows the versions. The Hebrew lacks the word, but it is doubtful whether the versions used a different text. The exclamatory force of "how" is largely a matter of representing the emphasis and the tone of voice.

(1:12–14)   [48] The girl speaks of, not to, the King; she is, therefore, speaking to the court ladies. She counters Solomon's doubtful compliment by referring directly to her all-absorbing attachment to her lover.

(1:12)   [49] "royal procession": The word used is in form a hiphîl participle (cf. Ps. 140:9) meaning, literally, "in his causing to go about." The finite hiphîl form is used of causing the ark to go in procession around a city in Josh. 6:11. Here our form may refer to the procession in and about Jerusalem in connection with Solomon's coronation ceremonies, glimpses of which are gotten in 1 Kings 1:38–40 and possibly also in the Song at 3:6 ff. (see notes 5 and 14). On this basis, the girl is saying that when the King was arrayed in his finest regalia and surrounded by all the pomp and splendor of the coronation procession she was thinking not of him but of her own lover.

[50] "Dodai": The reading of this word as a proper name re- (1:13) quires no change in the consonantal text. For the grounds for such a reading see Introduction, pp. 16–17. As the Song is arranged here, whether or not the form is a proper name has no particular effect upon the poem's interpretation as a whole. The choice of construction depends, therefore, solely on the probabilities in view of the use of the term in the Song. On its use with a suffix see note 89. Since the form *d o d* never means either "beloved" or "lover" outside the Song, there is no compulsion to follow the traditional rendering if an alternative is available. We may note on the one hand that there is no manifest reason why the girl should not name her lover, and, on the other, that since she seems to have tried to present as definite and concrete a picture of him as possible in other respects, both to the King and to the harem, there is a very natural motive for naming him. Since she felt obliged to portray her humble shepherd lover before the assembled court in contrast to Solomon, the portrayal would have been even more than normally difficult if she left her lover nameless.

There are, moreover, three places where the name seems to be demanded:

First, in 5:16, at the height of the girl's idealized description of her lover, it would be anticlimactic for her to say: "This is my lover and this is my friend." The omission of the name at this point would have been as inartistic as a life-size human statue without a face. In other words, we are here introduced to a vivid and striking personality. We know he was not nameless, and we have no right to assume that his name was not used unless there can be no doubt about it.

Second, in 5:9a, the reading "David" at the end of the line results in a manifest play on that name and the reference to the lover earlier in the same line. The term "David" can only refer to the royal house and is one of the greatest names in Israel. Since the importance of the two persons is being sharply contrasted, this is an ideal climax for the effective use of the lover's name.

Third, on the one occasion when the lover is present in person and the girl addresses him (8:14), if she wanted to use an epithet, since he is now more than a mere lover and she is alone with him, we might expect her to say "my betrothed" or even "my husband," but the simplest and most natural thing would be for her to call him by name.

In addition, while an epithet is entirely sufficient in Hebrew under any circumstances to designate an unmarried daughter, the language lacks precedent for referring to a man whose identity is known by any epithet that leaves his personal name out of account.

Finally, there is a compelling reason why the Judean editor of the Song could not allow the word to be read as a proper name (see Introduction, pp. 20 f.).

(1:14) [51] "Engedi": Engedi is an oasis, midway on the west coast of the Dead Sea, in the wilderness of Judea.

(1:15) [52] Solomon, disregarding the girl's remarks, repeats two earlier compliments (cf. 4:1).

(1:16—2:1) [53] The girl, taking her cue from the King's first compliment in 1:15, makes a touching apostrophe to her absent lover, whom she portrays as her future husband in their rural Northern home; she thereby reveals to both harem and King how the words of the latter serve only to focus her thoughts upon the absent shepherd, and she closes by again emphasizing her humble peasant character (2:1).

(1:16) [54] "nature's own greenness": The literal meaning is "fresh, green," but taken in connection with v. 17 the expression points to the green fields.

74

[55] "rafters": The Hebrew word is uncertain. (1:17)

[56] "rose": Literally, "meadow saffron" or "autumn crocus." (2:1)
What is meant is a flower as common as a wild rose.

[57] Solomon here makes a playful rejoinder at the expense (2:2)
of the harem.

[58] "Daughters": The Hebrew word is not a general term
meaning "maidens," as it is sometimes rendered, but is used
technically in the Song for the ladies of the harem; cf. 6:9de,
where "Daughters" and "queens and concubines" are definitely
equated. The girl herself always calls the ladies of the harem
"Daughters of Jerusalem." Thus the most distinguished daughters of the realm were before Solomon as he spoke. If he had
not meant to indicate them, there was no lack of other words
from which to choose.

[59] The girl, again taking her cue from Solomon's words, (2:3–7)
develops an analogous thought in relation to her lover, reflects
its emotional effect upon herself, and so leads up to her first
adjuration to the court ladies.

[60] "the sons": The Hebrew word means neither "youths," (2:3)
nor "young men," nor "men," but is a conscious antithesis to
"the Daughters" in v. 2, and thus means "among the most
distinguished."

[61] "the look in his eyes": Literally, "his gaze upon me." As (2:4)
G. B. Gray has shown (cf. "The Meaning of the Word *d e g e l*,"
Jewish Quarterly Review, 11 [1898]: 92 ff.), the traditional
rendering here of *d i g l o* as "banner" is extremely doubtful;
hence the rendering based upon Akkadian *d a g a l u*, "to look."

[62] The various adjurations challenge the court ladies' remarks (2:7)
in 1:3c and 1:4e, and thus show that the girl recognizes that
those lines refer to her as one of the servant girls; but she resents
their meaning in relation to herself because of her own lover.

[63] At this point the girl describes to the court a visit of her (2:8–17)
lover to her home in springtime. The phrase "the voice of

Dodai" occurs twice in the Song, and possibly in the original it occurred three times (cf. Introduction, p. 16). It is employed as a vivid means of describing the lover's presence reminiscently. It is as if she actually heard his voice.

(2:10)   [64] "sings": The usual rendering "spoke and said" or "speaks and says" is an attempt to treat poetically a well-known heavy, lumbering formula of late Hebrew prose, "he answered and said," often used where no one has as yet said anything. Here, however, we are dealing with a rare gem of lyric poetry; the whole poem is rightly called a song, and the expression in this instance is followed by three exquisite arias, vss. 10*b*–13, v. 14, and v. 15. There is no need, however, to try to help the writer to be poetical, for there is a perfectly good root of identical form that means "to sing."

  [65] "is calling": Literally, "says." This form of 'a m a r permits poetic treatment, and here, as the context shows, it means "is calling."

(2:17)   [66] "roam": Literally, "go round."

  [67] "rugged": The force of the Hebrew is uncertain. The literal meaning is "cutting"; LXX has "caverns."

(3:1–5)   [68] In 3:1–5 the girl describes her first dream after coming to Jerusalem (cf. 3:2–3) and utters her second adjuration.

The dream, told before the assembled court, serves the girl's purpose by emphasizing the pain and anxiety caused her by her separation from her lover, as well as her deep desire and intention to join him in her village home. Psychologically the dream reveals that in her mind there is as yet no insurmountable obstacle to prevent her from ultimately realizing her wish.

(3:1)   [69] This line follows the versions; the Hebrew omits it.

(4:7—5:2a)   [70] The reminiscence of the girl's second dream (cf. 5:2a) is told as a conversation with her lover and reflects a tradition about the girl from Shunem recorded in 1 Kings 2:17–24 (see Introduction, pp. 24, 29), namely, that Adonijah had asked for her as his bride. The dream develops out of the turmoil of queries that arose in her mind after this event. What would the shepherd lover say when he learned what had happened? Would he still trust her? What would he advise her to do? What would he say to the word "bride," which has been associated with her name at the palace? Would it turn his love against her?

[71] On the possible restoration in 4:7*a* of "The voice of Dodai" see Introduction, p. 16. Lines *bc* assure the girl that her lover still believes in her. (4:7)

[72] The reading "come" requires no change in the consonantal text. This is true also of "make an end" in the same line. (4:8)

[73] "Lebanon": The girl's dream fantasy plays upon the term, for she is in the palace called the "House of the Forest of Lebanon" (cf. 1 Kings 7:2). Her fears supply the wild beasts of that forest. The verse expresses her assurance that her lover would have her flee forthwith from such a dangerous place (cf. Introduction, p. 29).

[74] "Senir-Hermon": The compound name is connected by waw *explicativum*, equivalent to "Senir, that is, Hermon" (cf. Gesenius–Kautzsch, *op. cit.*, 154a, n. 1(b), and see Dt. 3:9).

[75] The word "bride" rings through vss. 9–15 like the fateful tolling of a bell. It has got beyond the girl's control, and it terrifies her. Her dream has expressed her private assurance that her lover still trusts her and that he would have her escape from her precarious position, but, that being so, what would he say and how address her? Realizing that the threat of "bride" to some prince has been hanging over her, so that he may lose her, indeed may already have lost her (cf. 2 Sam. 3:15–16), would he not put in words all that she has come to mean to him? The one thing he would not dare say now would be "my bride." But he could say "my sister," and he could and would say "bride," and hope for the best. Most in- (4:9–15)

terpreters have insisted on the rendering "my bride," and thereby have rejected one of the most superb poetic and dramatic psychological conceptions in literature.

(4:13)   [76] "whose [literally, 'your'] parting gifts": This rendering requires no change in the consonantal text; it belongs to the fountain figure that immediately precedes and that appears again in v. 15. Hence the traditional pointing which gives "shoots" or "products" is incorrect, for the fruits and spices do not grow out of a fountain, but come only from a garden. The pointing proposed, namely, *šilluḥe,* means "sending way," which is precisely what a fountain does with its waters; hence the meaning "parting gifts" when the fountain is personified, as here. The verse thus says that what the fountain sends forth is really all the fragrant and beautiful things that grow in the garden by reason of the life-giving waters. In other words, the waters make the garden (cf. v. 15).

The supplementary note in Field's *Hexapla* which assumes that *ek tou stomatos sou* is the equivalent of *šilluḥek* suggests, rather, an earlier displacement of two consonants that would give the reading *šilluḥe pîki,* that is, "the parting gift of your lips"; this would further heighten the personification and its figurative application to the girl (cf. v. 11*ab*). The figure is based upon a true oasis concept.

[77] "rows": *pardes* in the Hebrew text is a Semitic modification of a Persian word, a fact that carries a definite connotation as to date. There are, however, at least two main counts against its originality in the Song: (1) There is the variant text tradition *paradeisoi* of the Syro-Hexapla, which assumes a form ending in the plural; thus if the initial *p* of *pardes* were originally no part of the word (see preceding note), there would be left consonants that would readily yield *sidaroth,* "rows," which is suitable of pomegranates. (2) The passage 4:12–15 describes a walled-in garden with a fountain, and offers no

appropriate place for *pardes* in its original meaning "an extensive hunting park." LXX, as emphasized by Cannon (*op. cit.*, p. 131), was conscious of this difficulty when it left out the word for "pomegranates," since it could not conceive of a *pardes* of pomegranates. LXX also naturally balked at more than one such *pardes*. The Syro-Hexapla may have justified its plural by the many examples in the Song of the plural for the singular. But the accidental displacement of the two consonants *p* and *k* would account for all the phenomena, including the rise in the Persian period of *pardes* itself.

[78] The lofty and beautiful assurance of the shepherd's love (4:16) here calls forth the girl's glad response in terms of the garden figure of vss. 12 ff.

[79] The lover's reply picks up the thought in the preceding (5:1) lines and expresses his coming to his garden in terms of the wedding feast.

[80] The verbs in 5:1 are all to be taken as perfects of certainty. Most moderns, following the Masoretic pointing, read the last two verbs as imperatives. This procedure, however, throws the wedding scene entirely out of focus, since the appeal is then made to characters who have not yet been introduced.

[81] "kinsmen": *dod* means not only "uncle" but also "cousin" (cf. 1 Sam. 14:50) and, more generally, "kinsmen" (see Num. 36:11 and the corresponding LXX, which has *adelphoi* in parallel with "friends" in the line above).

[82] This line is not the introduction to line *b*, for the follow- (5:2*a*) ing reasons: (1) Line *b* in itself indicates a fresh topic (cf. the same situation in 2:8*a* and possibly in 4:7*a*). (2) To make line *a* introduce line *b* destroys the whole point of mentioning the voice, which is to present the lover vividly, as though actually present. (3) The girl's first dream has no such introduction, and the third is just as evidently a dream without it.

, Line *a* is suitable where it stands at the end of the second dream because of the dream's greater length and more intricate dramatic structure.

(5: 2*b*–8)   [83] The girl relates her third dream and follows it with her third adjuration.

(5: 3)   [84] The girl tells in 5: 3 of her inability, true to dream psychology, to do what she most desired.

(5:4)   [85] "to the latch": Literally, "from [i.e. 'outside'] the hole [of the door]."

(5: 6)   [86] "was not there": Based on Akkadian *d a b a r u;* the literal meaning is "went away." The girl's failure in the dream to find her lover reflects the deepening seriousness of her situation in her own mind. This is further reflected by the experiences recorded in v. 7.

(5:8)   [87] The three dreams, told consecutively, now bring their cumulative force to bear on the court ladies. This is manifest in the form of the adjuration, which the girl modifies to test the effect of the dreams by a direct appeal to the harem.

(5:9)   [88] The ladies' challenging reply shows that at last the girl has put them on the defensive. She has openly declared herself for marriage with a country shepherd rather than for membership in the royal harem. She has made comparisons, always to the advantage of the shepherd. She has even presumed to put the royal ladies under oath. And now she adroitly seeks to enlist their approval of her attitude! Their *amour-propre* is piqued. They will, once for all, put an end to this nonsense about "love" by making a crushing reply: "Really, what do you have in comparison?" The question affords her her greatest opportunity to show them, and she does this so effectively that she wins their open approval (see 6: 1).

[89] The proper names in 5: 9*a* are subtly and effectively used for contrast.

"your Dodai": This use of the name with the possessive sense has been challenged as improbable, but it is broadly and genuinely Semitic, as is seen, for example, in "my Damu" and "my Tammuz" in Babylonian liturgies (see S. Langdon, *Tammuz and Ishtar* [Philadelphia, 1919], *passim*), in "my Baal" in Hebrew (Hos. 2:16), and in the Syriac treatment of the present form. Its employment in the Song has a colloquial cast which is entirely justifiable, for the language is that used intimately within the harem and is analogous to the speech of any close group of young mothers today, who talk in similar vein of "your Charles" and "my James."

"David": On this reading see Introduction, p. 17. Though Solomon was now King, the royal house was never known by any other name than "David" (cf. 1 Kings 12:16, 19). The play, therefore, upon the words "Dod[a]i" and "David" was a natural and effective device to throw into sharpest contrast the disparity between Solomon and the shepherd.

⁹⁰ The girl answers the challenge of the court ladies with (5:10–16) an idealized portrait of her lover.

⁹¹ "full of luster": Literally, "sitting on fullness." (5:12)

⁹² "wafting": This agrees with LXX; the Hebrew has (5:13) "towers."

⁹³ "arms": Literally, "hands," i.e. what is at the sides. (5:14)

⁹⁴ "ivory work": Some form of ivory is intended, but the exact meaning is uncertain. .

⁹⁵ "sapphires": The Hebrew term used here is equivalent to Greek *sappheiros*, a blue gem also thought to be lapis lazuli.

⁹⁶ The ladies, charmed and fascinated by the portrayal of (6:1) the lover and momentarily forgetful of the presence of their lord and of their own station, express a desire to join the girl in search of the shepherd.

⁹⁷ The girl brings the ladies back to earth by assuring them (6:2–3)

that she has no doubt of the shepherd's whereabouts, and this permits her, in conclusion, to mention again in the hearing of the monarch her complete devotion to her lover.

(6:4-10) [98] In spite of the girl's winning the open sympathy and support of the harem and in spite of her many expressions of unbounded loyalty to the shepherd and love for him, Solomon renews his compliments and ends by recalling the occasion that first brought her to the attention of the court. It is noteworthy in this passage that, perhaps owing largely to her personal ability in winning the entire harem to her point of view, the maiden's stature has been greatly enhanced in the eyes of the King. He likens her in beauty to the two most important cities of Israel of the time, compares her in dignity to an army prepared for battle, and declares that he cannot look her in the eyes. It is also noteworthy that Solomon quickly runs out of compliments and heavily repeats himself.

(6:4) [99] "Tirzah": See Introduction, pp. 33, 37.

[100] "embattled host": Cf. LXX, "drawn up in order of battle."

(6:5c-7) [101] Compare 6:5c-7 with 4:1d-3. At the end of 6:7 the Hebrew adds "behind your veil"; see note 18.

(6:8) [102] This is the first time the King has deigned to recognize openly the presence of the harem, and he does so here simply to impress upon the girl that she is *the* one, while they are so many; but naturally the argument defeats itself, as the author undoubtedly intended it should.

(6:9) [103] "One": The meaning requires that "of them" be supplied in thought, for the court ladies had indicated that the girl was a servant (see note 33), and she had not questioned this classification (see note 62). The King, moreover, says nothing to show that this is not so, nor does he offer her any change of status. Even when he emphasizes the fact that she is an only one, he does not commit himself, for he is very careful to refer

that estimate to her mother. And this remark itself seems
to be a striving for effect, since we know that she had at least
two older brothers, and hence it could mean merely that she
was an only daughter, which was always a very doubtful compliment in the Near East.

[104] On the equivalence of "Daughters" (in the preceding line)
with "queens and concubines" see note 58. Lines *de* describe
the occasion when the girl first came to the attention of members
of the court (see Introduction, p. 25).

[105] "like the blush of dawn": Literally, "who looks forth (6:10)
like the dawn."

[106] The girl explains how she happened to meet the royal (6:11–12)
retinue.

[107] "fresh growth": For the usage cf. Job 8: 12. (6:11)

[108] "fancy": Literally, "soul" or "desire." (6:12)

[109] "brought": Literally, "put, set."

[110] "princely": The reference is to representatives of the
royal household; see Introduction, p. 25, and cf. Ehrlich, *op.
cit.*, p. 15.

[111] Members of the harem repeat words they spoke on first (6:13*ab*)
seeing the girl.

[112] "stay": The literal meaning is "turn" or "return," but
here the ladies of the harem are only asking the girl not to run
away; cf. Ehrlich, *op. cit.*, p. 15.

[113] "Shunammite": LXX (B text) has this reading. The
Hebrew and Greek S and A texts read "Shulammite." Shunem
was the older name of present-day Shulem. The B text has
the older form of the name, which is found also in 1 Kings 1: 3.
It is easy to see why the older form might be changed to that
of later times, but, in view of the history of the Song's interpretation, there is no cogent reason to expect a change in the opposite
direction. A deeper question is: Is the earliest form of the
Song, as it is dated on other grounds, early enough to have

known only the older form of the name?   On the dating of the
Song see Introduction, pp. 33 f.

(6:13cd)   [114] The girl here recalls her protest when she first met the
harem.

[115] "dance of two companies": This may refer to a traditional
war dance between two armies before they joined battle.   In
any case, the figure is hyperbolic, and there is no evidence that
the girl had actually danced.

(7:1-5)   [116] The ladies praise the maiden's physical beauty as she
appeared on the day they met her, but the scene is adroitly
shifted to the present and reconstructed as though taking place
before the King.

(7:1)   [117] "sandals": The girl was very likely barefoot at the time.

(7:2)   [118] "body": The meaning is obscure.   The Hebrew has
"navel"; the term was perhaps used for the lower abdomen.

[119] "waist": Literally, "belly."   The term may have indicated the upper abdomen.

(7:5)   [120] "crowns": Literally, "is upon."

[121] "tresses": The Hebrew is uncertain.

(7:6-9a)   [122] The King makes his final approaches.

(7:7)   [123] "You are stately as": Literally, "This your stature is
like."

(7:8)   [124] "breath": Literally, "nose."

(7:9a)   [125] "kisses": Literally, "palate."

(7:9b—8:4)   [126] The lines that follow express the girl's open rebuff of the
King and her unflinching loyalty to her lover; they end with
her final adjuration to the harem.

(7:9bc)   [127] "flowing": Literally, "going."

[128] "as is his right": Literally, "according to right."

[129] "gliding over": That is, slowly and gently, for full en-
joyment of the flavor.

[130] "lips and teeth": This rendering follows the versions;
the Hebrew has "lips of the sleepers."

84

[131] "O that we might": This is a cohortative conditioned (7:11) by the fact that the lover is still not present (cf. 8: 1c).

[132] "token": This interpretation results from reading '*o th* (7:12) for '*e th*, with no change of the basic text. The token would consist of the mandrakes (love apples) they would find, but, more especially, of the choice fruits the girl had laid up with her own hands for use in their future home (cf. v. 13).

[133] "O that you were": Literally, "who will give you." (8:1)

[134] "in the street": Literally, "without."

[135] "who was ever my instructor": This is a frequentative (8:2) imperfect. The versions read: "and unto the chamber of her that conceived me," which repeats 3: 4e. The repetition is not needed, but its rejection leaves the expression given here, which is the more difficult reading, to be accounted for. The form is, furthermore, not one that a later hand could be expected to have supplied. The reading does, however, serve a real function. The spiced wine and the wine of pomegranates in the next two lines, as well as the choice fruits (7: 13) which represent the work of the girl's own hands, are now found in the house of her mother, whom she credits with teaching her to be a good housewife. This intimate domestic touch, as well as her reliance on her mother, is characteristic of the heroine (cf. 3: 4); and it removes any taint of eroticism, such as is often assumed to be present in her motivation.

[136] The question here records the girl's astonishment at the (8:4) outcome of the whole situation; it marks the psychological culmination and climax of the entire scene.

The adjurations as a whole are a striking phenomenon and are handled with great adroitness and dramatic skill. The very fact that a humble peasant girl should thus put under oath the entire harem, whose sixty queens were reputed for the most part to be foreign princesses, was in itself startlingly dramatic. Her action was warranted by her personal relation to King

David, by the acknowledgment of the ladies of the harem themselves that she was the most beautiful among women, and by the undivided attention shown her by the King in the presence of the harem, to say nothing of the importance she had derived from the request of the ill-fated Adonijah.

In form, the adjurations are a rejoinder to the remarks of the court ladies in 1:2–4 (cf. Introduction, pp. 12 f.), but even as early as the first one it is evident that the girl has in mind an emotion much more real and vital than any possible love for Solomon. By the time of the second her vivid reminiscence of the shepherd lover makes it clear that the adjuration has shifted completely from any thought of Solomon and is concerned only with the absent lover. The third adjuration openly focuses on the shepherd lover. And the last one is little more than an exclamation of astonishment that the ladies of the harem, by their attitude, their actions, and their words, have provided the setting and the stimuli for drawing from her an open confession, in the presence of the King, of her undying love and her unyielding devotion to her betrothed. What follows is the denouement, on which both the book of Kings and the Song agree. According to the former, she did not enter the harem; according to the latter, she not only did not enter the harem but actually returned to her native village and rejoined her shepherd lover. The account of their reunion is given in Part II of the Song (8:5–14).

(8:5ab) [137] The girl's brothers observe a woman approaching the village accompanied by Dodai. At a distance they recognize him but not her and are scandalized at the thought that their sister has been so quickly replaced by a stranger.

[138] "Who is that": Cf. 3:6 and see Introduction, p. 22.

[139] "wilderness": The girl is pictured making her way home, probably by the Jordan Valley route.

[140] "arm in arm": Literally, "leaning upon." The recipro-

cal force of the hithpael accurately describes the approaching lovers.

¹⁴¹ "Dodo": The reading of the pointed text, "Dodah," follows the assumption of the Judean editor that the name is only an epithet for Solomon. However, the unpointed text very naturally ends in *o* with final *h,* as does the Hebrew of the name "Solomon." Furthermore, elsewhere both "Dodai" and "Dodo," appear in the same verse (2 Sam. 23:9), and the same person is called "Dodai" in 1 Chron. 27:4 and "Dodo" in 1 Chron. 11:12. How the name came to have the variant spelling and pronunciation is now hidden from us, but the indication is that "Dodai" is earlier; a clue to the later use may be found in the present passage. The name is here in emphatic form. Such occasional emphatic pronunciation may have led to the exclusive use of this form to designate certain persons.

The person mentioned here in 8:5*b* is apparently well known to the brothers of the girl, and is, indeed, one of her childhood friends, for he recalls how he awakened her one day under an old apple tree they are now approaching and then points out her mother's home as the place where she was born. The writer thus quite probably regarded him as a native Shunammite, although this is not explicit.

¹⁴² The conversation of the approaching lovers is overheard (8:5*c–e*) as Dodai points out the girl's home.

¹⁴³ "Yonder, etc.": Literally, "There your mother was pregnant with you, there she was pregnant who bore you."

¹⁴⁴ The lines that follow are a panegyric to triumphant love. (8:6–12)

¹⁴⁵ "ardent love": The meaning "jealousy" (American Revised Version) is inappropriate here, since what is referred to is the emotion that characterizes the lovers and that is represented as the cause of their triumph. Jealousy nowhere enters the picture. And the emotion is more than physical passion. The term in question is used in a good sense of zeal for the

87

Lord (2 Kings 10: 16) and zeal for the house of God (cf. Ps. 69: 9). Here it indicates a sentiment that surpasses ordinary human love in depth and intensity.

[146] "consuming fire": Literally, "a flame of Yah." "Yah" is a shortened form of "Yahweh" and first appears in early Hebrew poetry. This is the only occurrence of a divine name in the Song, and here it is used to express a superlative, i.e. "the mightiest flame."

(8: 7)　　[147] This line may also be rendered: "Would men at all despise him?" The question requires no particular sign. The answer would be "No, because men know that love is more valuable than material wealth." According to the present rendering, men utterly despise such efforts because love is priceless.

(8: 8-9)　　[148] The girl recalls, in vss. 8-9, her brothers' remarks about her as a child in order to explain her triumphant return (see note 149).

(8: 10)　　[149] "Wall" (line *a*) and "towers" are here used figuratively of the girl's successful defense of her personal freedom against Solomon's efforts to include her in the royal harem.

(8: 11)　　[150] "has": The verb is perfect, but is used of what is still true (cf. v. 12*bc*).

(8: 12)　　[151] This line rounds out the dramatic motif introduced at 1: 6*e*.

(8: 13)　　[152] The lover asks the maiden for a song.

[153] "garden": Literally, "gardens." The plural is here used for the singular, as often in the Song.

(8: 14)　　[154] The girl playfully sings in response to her lover's request.
[155] "fragrant": Literally, "spices."